# IMAGES OF WAR

# M7 PRIEST HMC

## RARE PHOTOGRAPHS FROM WARTIME ARCHIVES

### David Doyle

Pen & Sword
**MILITARY**

First published in Great Britain in 2019 by
**PEN & SWORD MILITARY**
An imprint of
Pen & Sword Books Ltd
47 Church Street
Barnsley
South Yorkshire
S70 2AS

ISBN 978-1-52673-885-1

A CIP catalogue record for this book is available from the British Library.

Typeset by Concept, Huddersfield, West Yorkshire HD4 5JL
Printed and bound in Europe by Printworks Global Ltd

Pen & Sword Books Limited incorporates the imprints of Atlas, Archaeology, Aviation, Discovery,
Family History, Fiction, History, Maritime, Military, Military Classics, Politics, Select, Transport,
True Crime, Air World, Frontline Publishing, Leo Cooper, Remember When, Seaforth Publishing,
The Praetorian Press, Wharncliffe Local History, Wharncliffe Transport, Wharncliffe True Crime
and White Owl.

For a complete list of Pen & Sword titles please contact
PEN & SWORD BOOKS LIMITED
47 Church Street, Barnsley, South Yorkshire S70 2AS, England
E-mail: enquiries@pen-and-sword.co.uk
Website: www.pen-and-sword.co.uk

# Contents

# Acknowledgements

This book would not have been possible without a great deal of help from a number of friends and institutions, including the late Richard Hunnicutt and Fred Crismon. Also extremely helpful were Tom Kailbourn, Scott Taylor, Pat Stansell, Jim Gilmore and Dana Bell. As with all of my books, none of this would have happened without the constant help and encouragement of my wonderful wife Denise.

# Introduction

While the US Army had made efforts to create self-propelled artillery in the waning days of the First World War, these efforts quickly stagnated following the signing of the Armistice. While hundreds of the armed vehicles had been ordered, only a few were completed prior to the end of hostilities and the subsequent cancellations.

Apart from a few experimental pieces, many based on the First World War-conceived vehicle, little effort was made by the United States to mechanize artillery until war broke out in Europe for a second time in 1939.

When the Armored Force was created in 1940, the table of organization and equipment called for an armored field artillery regiment to be a component of each armored division. To fulfill this requirement, many units were equipped with the M2 half-track towing a M1897 75mm gun. However, when Army Chief of Staff General George C. Marshall appointed Major General Jacob Devers as the second Chief of the Armored Force in August 1941, the shape of American artillery began to undergo rapid changes.

While the Chief of the Armored Force for the first year of its existence was Adna Chaffee, whose chosen branch of service was cavalry, Devers had selected artillery as his branch upon graduation from West Point in 1909. Just one month after Devers' appointment a request for authorization to construct a 105mm Howitzer Motor Carriage was issued, and denied by the adjutant general. The next month the decision was reversed, and in October the Ordnance Committee began development of that vehicle.

Devers had advocated that this vehicle be based on the chassis of the M3 medium tank and two prototypes, designated T32, were ordered from Baldwin Locomotive Works. Owing to concerns about the development and production process, work also began on the half-track-based 105mm Howitzer Motor Carriage T19.

The Baldwin T32 featured an M2A1 105mm Howitzer as well as the top portion of its field carriage mounted inside an open-topped, box-like superstructure atop the M3 chassis. The two prototypes were shipped to Aberdeen Proving Ground, where trials indicated that some modifications were in order. Foremost of these was the lowering of the rear armor panel of the fighting compartment in order to facilitate the servicing of the piece and the cleaning of the breech.

The slightly modified first prototype, W-6010106, was then shipped to the Armored Force Board at Fort Knox for evaluation. These tests were conducted from

5 February 1942 through 8 February 1942. The tests concluded that while the T32 was superior to the T19 (which had begun testing in November 1941), further modification of the T32 design was in order.

The board recommended that the frontal armor be raised by 3in for increased protection, while at the same time advocating that the side armor be lowered by 11in to ease servicing the piece. Perhaps even more significant, the traverse of the howitzer in the T32 was 15 degrees right and 23 degrees left, but the board wanted the 15-degree left and 30-degree right traverse as offered by the standard field carriage. Aesthetically, the most significant change was the board's request that a .50 caliber anti-aircraft machine gun be mounted either on a pintle at the rear of the vehicle or via a ring mount in a forward corner of the fighting compartment.

Technicians at Aberdeen Proving Ground modified the second prototype so that the requests of the Armored Force Board were met, including opting for the forward-mounted anti-aircraft ring mount, which would serve as the inspiration for the vehicle's name 'Priest'. The modified second prototype was then shipped to the American Locomotive Company (ALCO) in Schenectady, New York to serve as a model for the 600 vehicles of the type the firm had been contracted to produce.

Deliveries of production vehicles began in March 1942 when the first two off the assembly line were shipped to Aberdeen for evaluation. One was used for automotive tests, while the other was used by the Design Section for a stowage study. That study resulted in further minor changes to the design, beginning on 5 May 1942 when ammunition stowage was increased from fifty-seven to sixty-nine rounds, in part by eliminating two folding crew seats from the fighting compartment. In April 1942 the modified T32 was standardized as the M7 105mm Howitzer Motor Carriage.

As production neared the 100-vehicle mark, several changes were made to the rear of the vehicle. While initially the rear was very similar to that of the M3 medium tank, the improved vehicles had relocated engine air filters and mufflers, as well as the addition of armored vent covers on the engine deck as an aid to venting gasoline fumes.

By July 1942, after about 200 vehicles had been completed, a change was made to the tops of the rear stowage bins. Originally configured to accept external auxiliary fuel tanks, similar to those used on M3 Stuart tanks, the tops of the stowage bins featured the appropriate mounting hardware. Once this plan was abandoned, the now superfluous brackets were eliminated. This also would allow the boxes, by August, to become top-opening rather than side-opening. Also during the summer of 1942, the so-called step in the three-piece transmission housing, necessary to accommodate the 75mm mount of the M3 medium tank upon which the M7 was based, was eliminated and the notch-free three-piece transmission housing of the M4 medium tank was adopted instead.

Also used briefly during the summer of 1942 production was the one-piece transmission housing produced by Caterpillar. However, this transmission assembly was in considerable demand for M4 tank production, which along with other factors drove the bulk of M7 production to continue to use the three-piece transmission housing.

The M7 first saw combat in the hands of the British in North Africa, arriving in September 1942, and it was the British who gave the vehicle its code-name Priest. Those combat experiences, as well as those of US troops involved in Operation TORCH two months later, led to further changes in the M7 form. Beginning in January 1943, the pulpit – the curved armor beneath the ring mount – was extended further down the side of the vehicle, allowing the gunner to sit in this area. Also, in effect reversing the earlier decision to lower the sides of the fighting compartment, folding side panes were developed for the sides and rear, increasing the protection of the stowed ammunition.

Between April 1942 and August 1943, the American Locomotive Company built 2,814 of these self-propelled guns on contract W-740-ORD-485. The vehicles were given the Standard Nomenclature List (SNL) designation G-128.

Experience in battle showed room for improvement, and in the period March through October 1944, the ALCO contract W-740-ORD-485 was extended to include a further 500 vehicles. These vehicles can be distinguished from the earlier production models by means of the single-piece E8543 transmission cover, baskets affixed to the tops of the sponson stowage boxes and more robust suspension. However, as with their predecessors, these vehicles retained the Continental R975 C1 nine-cylinder radial engine.

By this time, however, the US Army had begun to prefer the V-8 Ford model GAA engine for the tank fleet, and not surprisingly wanted the self-propelled howitzer to use the same engine. Accordingly a contract was issued to the Pressed Steel Car Company to produce such a vehicle, designated the M7B1. The rear of the vehicle was redesigned accordingly, and deliveries of the new vehicle began in March 1944. Two contracts were issued with Pressed Steel for these vehicles, with production of 826 vehicles being completed in February 1945. Reflecting the change in power plant, the vehicles were categorized as SNL G-199.

Strangely, additional Continental-powered M7 vehicles were ordered from the Federal Machine and Welder Company in June 1944. Deliveries of these vehicles began in March 1945 and 176 were built before the contract was terminated in July 1945.

The rugged terrain of Korea again showcased the shortcomings of the 35-degree upper elevation limit of the Priest. To increase the elevation of the howitzer for better use in such conditions, during the 1950s a program was initiated to raise the upper elevation limit to 65 degrees, coincidentally the same upper limit as found on the prototype T32 in 1942. At that time planners thought that a lower profile was of greater importance than increased elevation, and mandated the change that resulted in the M7 and M7B1 having a 35-degree elevation. This meant that in combat conditions oftentimes the vehicles were positioned on slopes or constructed ramps in order to raise the effective elevation.

Rather than these expedient means, the new program converted 127 M7B1 vehicles to the M7B2 configuration. This modification meant utilizing a taller, modified gun mount, with a similar change to the machine-gun ring. All this resulted in a very different façade for the vehicle.

The Priest was used by British, Canadian and US forces in Europe, and by the US Army and Marines in the Pacific during the Second World War. Remaining in the US Army inventory into the 1950s, the Priest was again called into action in Korea. The vehicle continued to serve in the hands of Allied nations into the 1970s.

# Chapter One

# Baldwin Locomotive Works T32

By the autumn of 1941, the US Army had set out on a course to develop a fully-tracked, self-propelled 105mm howitzer: a vehicle capable of keeping up with armored forces and delivering substantial firepower. Towards that end, the Baldwin Locomotive Works was tasked with constructing two pilot vehicles with the 105mm Howitzers M2A1 mounted on Medium Tank M3 chassis. These vehicles were designated the 105mm Howitzer Motor Carriage T32, one of which is seen here undergoing testing at the Baldwin Locomotive Works plant. (*Baldwin Locomotive Works*)

On the 105mm Howitzer Motor Carriage T32, the howitzer was mounted slightly to the right of the longitudinal centerline of the chassis. The superstructure to the front of the engine compartment was totally reworked to form a fighting compartment that was protected on the front, sides and rear by 0.75in welded armor plates. The driver sat on the left side of the howitzer. (*Baldwin Locomotive Works*)

The superstructure from the rear of the fighting compartment to the rear of the vehicle was substantially the same as that of the Medium Tank M3, with riveted armor-plate construction and, on top, a ventilation grille, armored covers for the fuel-filler caps and removable engine-access plates. (*Baldwin Locomotive Works*)

(**Above**) One of two 105mm Howitzer Motor Carriages T32 is seen from the rear as it performs a climbing test at the Baldwin Locomotive plant. The fighting compartment was open-topped, which would leave the crew vulnerable to artillery airbursts and overhead fire. (*Baldwin Locomotive Works*)

(**Opposite, above**) The 105mm Howitzer M2A1 on the T32 was equipped with a curved armored shield that traversed in unison with the howitzer. However, the total traverse of the piece was limited to 31 degrees. (*Baldwin Locomotive Works*)

(**Opposite, below**) In this photo the 105mm Howitzer M2A1 is traversed to the right. Because of the location of the howitzer and its mount, the driver's position and vision port were moved further to the left than in the Medium Tank M3. (*Baldwin Locomotive Works*)

The Ordnance Department tested both of the pilot 105mm Howitzer Motor Carriages T32 at Aberdeen Proving Ground, Maryland. The first pilot T32, US Army registration number (hereafter 'registration number') W-6010106, is seen here in a 23 January 1942 photograph. The driver had a front and a side hinged visor with a Protectoscope, a viewing device with a block of armored glass. The driver's front port is fitted here with a windshield with a wiper and wiper motor. (*Patton Museum*)

The first pilot T32, left, is compared with a Medium Tank M3 at Aberdeen Proving Ground on 24 January 1942. The armor of the T32's fighting compartment was simplified, featuring a single vertical rear plate instead of the three rear plates (the outer two of which were angled) of the Medium Tank M3. Three ladder rungs were welded to each side of the T32 for ease of crew access. (*National Archives & Records Administration, hereafter NARA*)

A small number 1 was painted on the lower front corner of the side plate of the first pilot T32. The bogie assemblies were the stock vertical-volute units as used on early M3 medium tanks, with five-spoked bogie wheels and the track-support rollers mounted at the top of the bogie frames. The sprockets were the thirteen-spoked D47366 type. The idler wheels were six-spoked. *(NARA)*

The second pilot 105mm Howitzer Motor Carriage T32, registration number 6010107, wore a white number 2 on the lower front corner of the side armor of the fighting compartment. When photographed at Aberdeen Proving Ground on 29 January 1942, this vehicle was virtually indistinguishable from the first pilot, but this would soon change. *(NARA)*

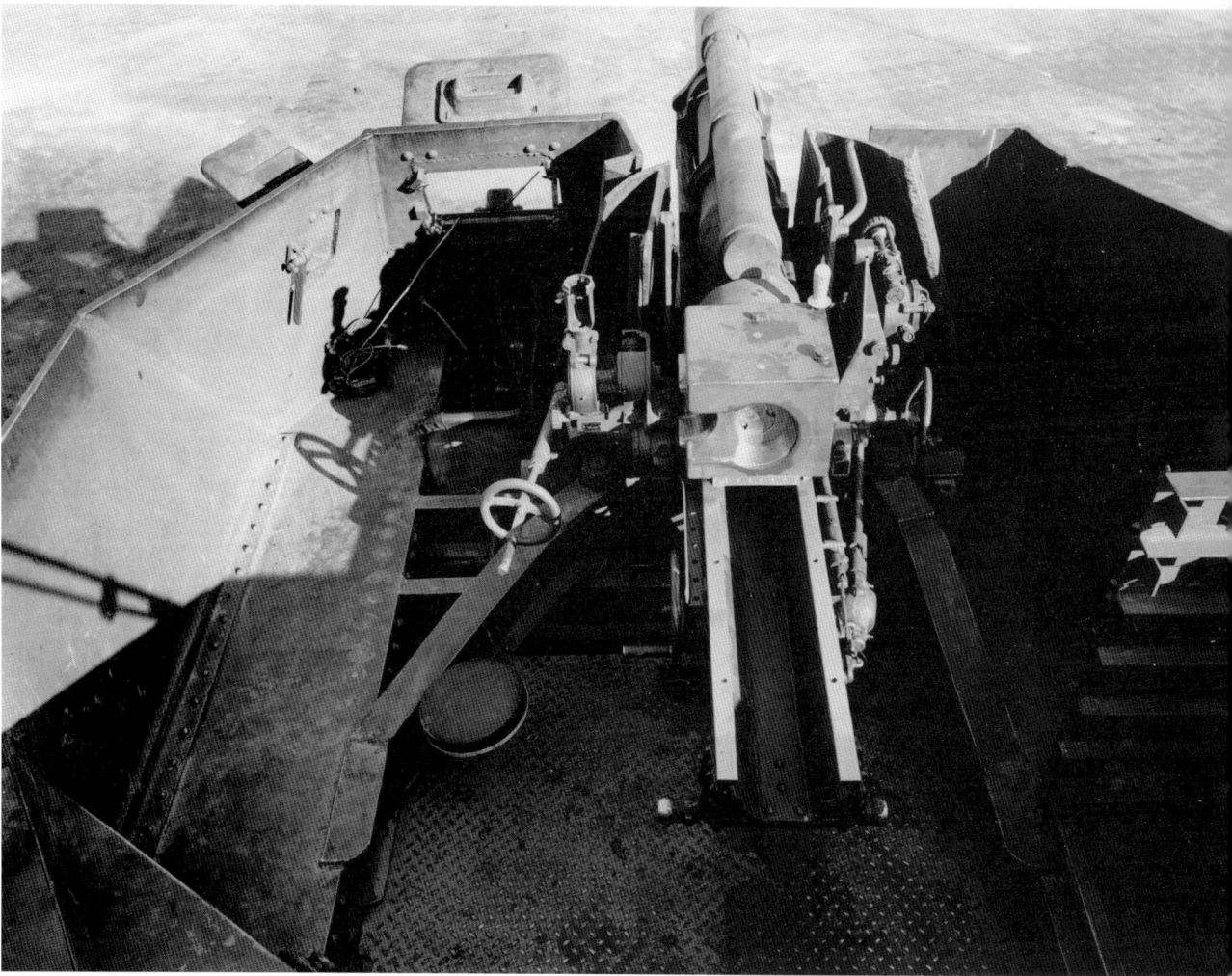

(**Above**) The interior of one of the 105mm Howitzer Motor Carriages T32 is viewed from the rear deck. The howitzer and its carriage were installed on a support structure that included two I-beam braces, to help stabilize the piece and distribute the force of recoil when the howitzer was fired. The driver sat to the front left of the mount, with no overhead protection. The rack to the right presumably was for storing ammunition. The T32, as built, could carry forty-four rounds of 105mm ammunition. (*NARA*)

(**Opposite, above**) A crew is serving the 105mm howitzer on the first pilot T32, registration number W-6010106, during firing tests of the vehicle for the Armored Force Board at Fort Knox, Kentucky in 1942. The right side of the curved, movable shield for the howitzer is visible; it was designed to fit tightly against the fixed frontal armor of the fighting compartment. (*NARA*)

(**Opposite, below**) A GI hands a round of 105mm ammunition to another soldier in the first pilot 105mm Howitzer Motor Carriage T32 during firing tests at Fort Knox in 1942. In the foreground are 105mm ammunition crates and a pile of fiberboard packing tubes for individual rounds. (*NARA*)

U.S.A. W-6010106

(**Above**) To improve the operational serviceability of the 105mm Howitzer Motor Carriage T32, personnel at Aberdeen Proving Ground modified the armor of the second pilot vehicle. As seen in a 1 March 1942 photo at a shop at Aberdeen, the personnel eliminated the angled plate to the left of the driver's frontal armor by welding in plates to extend the frontal armor and the side armor so that they met. The upper rear part of the side armor of the fighting compartment was cut down by 11in (thus eliminating the top ladder rung). A 3in-high sloping structure was welded to the armor above the driver's compartment, and a ring mount for a machine gun was installed to the right of the howitzer. (*NARA*)

(**Opposite, above**) As seen in a view from the left rear of the modified second pilot T32, the angled right front of the superstructure was cut out, and a revamped structure was substituted below and to the front of the ring mount. Eliminating the angled facets from the superstructure yielded more interior space. (*NARA*)

(**Opposite, below**) Following successful testing of the T32s, the second pilot vehicle was delivered to the American Locomotive Works, Schenectady, New York for use as the model for developing a production version designated the 105mm Howitzer Motor Carriage M7 that was authorized for production. The first production M7, registration number W-3034235, was tested at Aberdeen Proving Ground, as shown in an 8 April 1942 photograph. At this point, the headlight assemblies lacked brush guards. (*Patton Museum*)

(**Above**) The M7's superstructure as seen from the left side generally followed the lines of the modified, second prototype T32, with the frontal and side armor sections joining at right angles, and the cut-outs in the upper rear areas of the side armor of the fighting compartment. Storage containers had been added to the tops of the sponsons. (*NARA*)

(**Opposite, above**) The ring mount for the 105mm Howitzer Motor Carriage M7, sometimes called the 'pulpit', was installed on a semi-cylindrical armored casting that was welded to the top of the fighting compartment side armor. The ring mount was intended for a Browning .50-caliber M2 HB machine gun, for use principally in anti-aircraft defense. (*NARA*)

(**Opposite, below**) As seen in an 8 April 1942 photo of the first production M7 at Aberdeen, the machine-gun ring mount jutted out of the right of the side armor of the fighting compartment, casting a shadow on that plate. The bogie assemblies remained the early-type vertical-volute design with the track-support rollers above the top of the bogie frames. (*NARA*)

(**Above**) The 105mm Howitzer M2A1 as installed on a Mount M4 in the M7 had a traverse of 30 degrees to the right and 15 degrees to the left for a total traverse of 45 degrees; a substantial improvement over the T32's howitzer's total traverse of 31 degrees. A soldier demonstrates aiming the machine gun at 90 degrees right traverse. The slanted panel above the driver's compartment provided him with a bit of protection from overhead fire and shell bursts. The final drive assembly (abbreviated to FDA, the armored bow that enclosed the final drive) of the earliest M7s were the same type used on the Medium Tank M3, distinguished by a slight recess on its top-right edge. On the top of the right-hand section of the FDA, there is one bolt on the raised top edge and four bolts on the recessed part of the edge. (*NARA*)

(**Opposite, above**) This Aberdeen Proving Ground photo of the driver's compartment of an M7 in late April 1942 shows the various stowage brackets and racks installed. Marked on the photo were the locations of equipment and supplies to be stowed in the compartment. For example, on the left sidewall were brackets for a Thompson sub-machine gun, four Protectoscope prisms, a .30-caliber rifle and a first-aid kit. (*NARA*)

(**Opposite, below**) A 15 April 1942 Aberdeen Proving Ground photo documents the locations of stowed equipment in the rear of the fighting compartment and on the rear deck of an M7. There were two bins in the rear corners of the compartment, each of which held twelve rounds of 105mm ammunition in their fiberboard packing tubes. Eight rounds of 105mm ammunition are visible in a bin under the floor towards the lower right. (*NARA*)

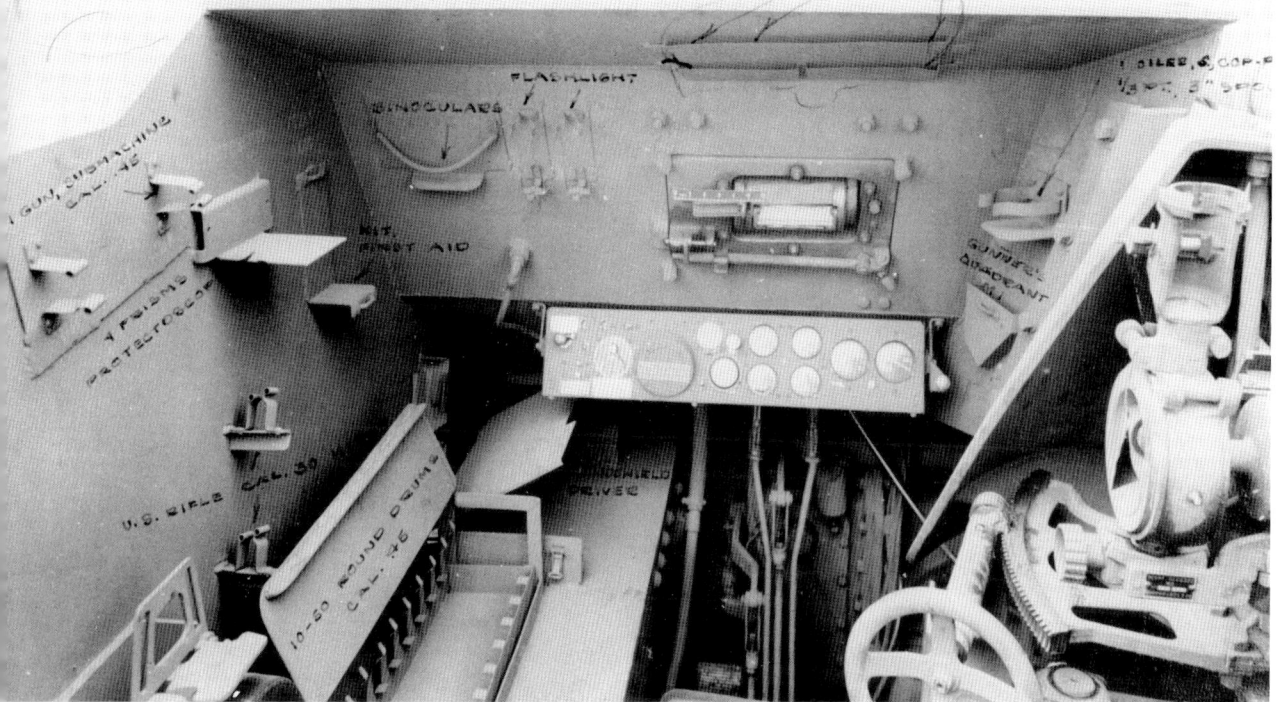

MANUAL, TECHNICAL, TM9
1 BOOK, ORDNANCE
(NOTEM) FORM 7255

1 BOOK, ARTY GUN, O.O.
FORM 5825 - BLANK 7

CHECK - CHART, LUBRICATION
GUIDE № 52

CHECK - CHART, LUBRICATION
GUIDE № C

1 OILER, S, COP-R
1/3 PT, 3" SEC

1 GUN, SUBMACHINE
CAL 45

1 PRISM
PROTECTOSCOPE

BINOCULARS

FLASHLIGHT

KIT,
FIRST AID

GUNNERS
QUADRANT
M1

U.S. RIFLE CAL 30

10-20 ROUND DRUMS
CAL 45

WINDSHIELD
DRIVER

PICK HANDLE

RESTRICTED

TOW CABLE

SHOVEL

CROWBAR

12 RDS.
105 MM
HOWITZER
AMMO.

12 RDS.
105 MM
HOWITZER
AMMO.

FLASHLITE

FLASHLITE

TRAVELING
LOCK

UNLOADING
RAMMER
BRACKET

8 RDS.
105 MM
HOWITZER
AMMO.

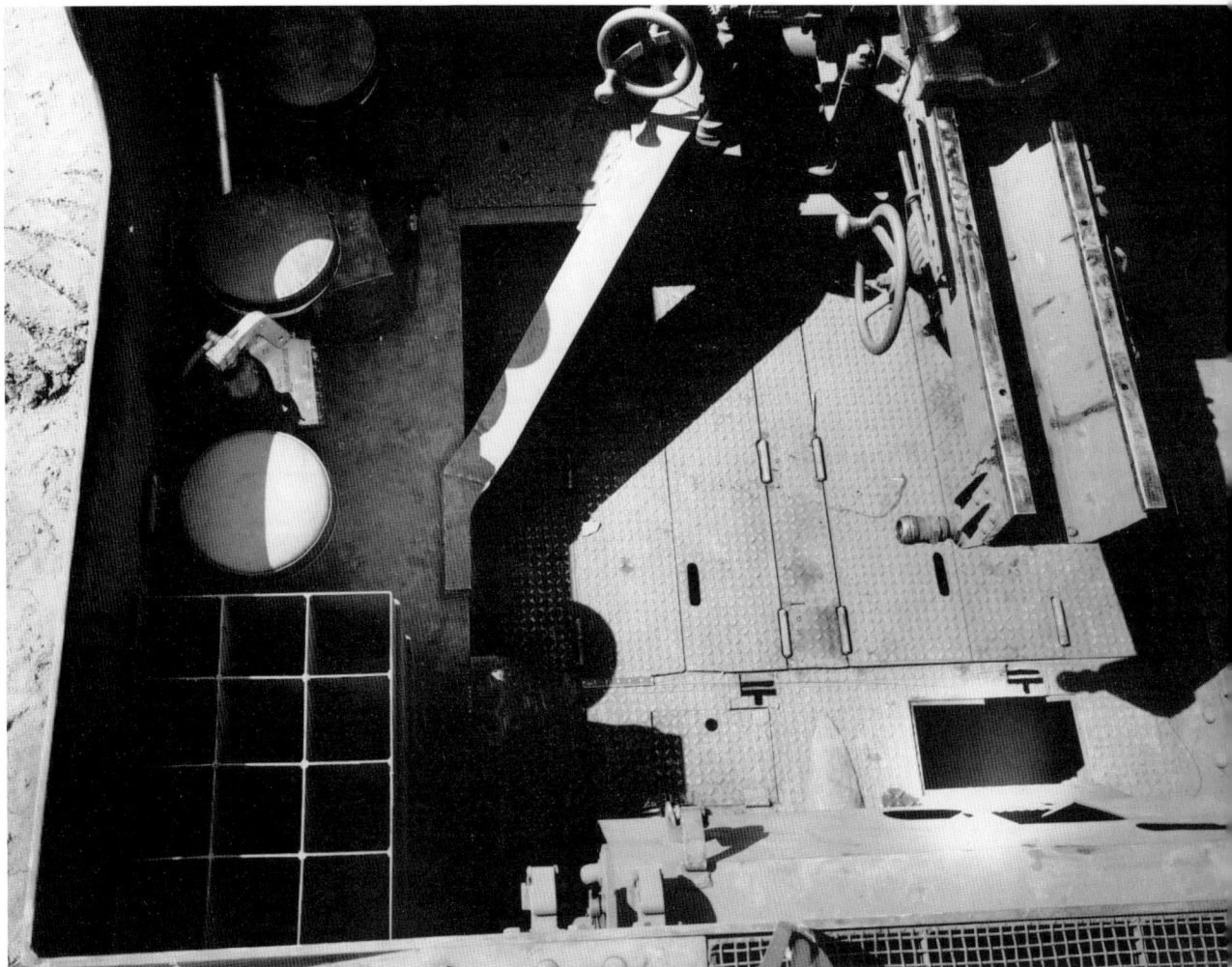

(**Above**) The rear of the fighting compartment is viewed from above the front of the deck over the engine compartment. To the left side are three crew seats. The lower part of the floor between the sponsons was fabricated from diamond-tread steel plate, with various hinged access doors for stowage compartments below the floor. (*NARA*)

(**Opposite, above**) The door to a stowage compartment under the floor of an M7's fighting compartment is open; this compartment held nine rounds of 105mm ammunition. On the right sidewall are two crew seats. The 105mm howitzer is traversed to approximately its full right limit of 30 degrees. (*NARA*)

(**Opposite, below**) The fourth M7 is seen from above at Aberdeen Proving Ground on 7 May 1942. Two bows for supporting a tarpaulin over the fighting compartment are installed. On the rear deck, running fore and aft, are four raised metal strips which formed a rack for stowing the tarpaulin. The stowage boxes on top of the sponsons are the early type with a door on the outboard side, with two hinges at the bottom and a padlock hasp at the top. Atop each of the boxes are brackets and fittings for mounting an auxiliary fuel tank. (*NARA*)

(**Above**) In a view of M7 serial number 3 at Aberdeen on 11 July 1942, one of the tarpaulin bows is stowed on brackets on the right side of the fighting compartment. Below the bow, stowed in brackets and secured with a strap, are four tubes that would be assembled into two supports for the bow. (*NARA*)

(**Opposite, above**) The purpose of this photo of the fighting compartment of a 105mm Howitzer Motor Carriage M7 taken at Aberdeen on 28 May 1942 was to demonstrate the method of removing the canvas cover from the breech. The cover had a heavy-duty zipper running fore-and-aft on its top. The object lying laterally across the zipper was a ruler. At the rear of the howitzer cradle, at the bottom of the photo, is the travel lock for the howitzer. Shortly after M7 production began, the folding crew seats would be removed to make room for a single row of extra ammunition bins on each side of the fighting compartment. (*NARA*)

(**Opposite, below**) In a close-up view of the front right corner of the fighting compartment of an early-production M7, at the top is a flashlight and at the lower center is a toolbox drawer, with a tray for .50-caliber ammunition boxes above it. To the right of the tray is a collapsible canvas bucket. Below the gun mount to the left are two 5-gallon liquid containers. (*NARA*)

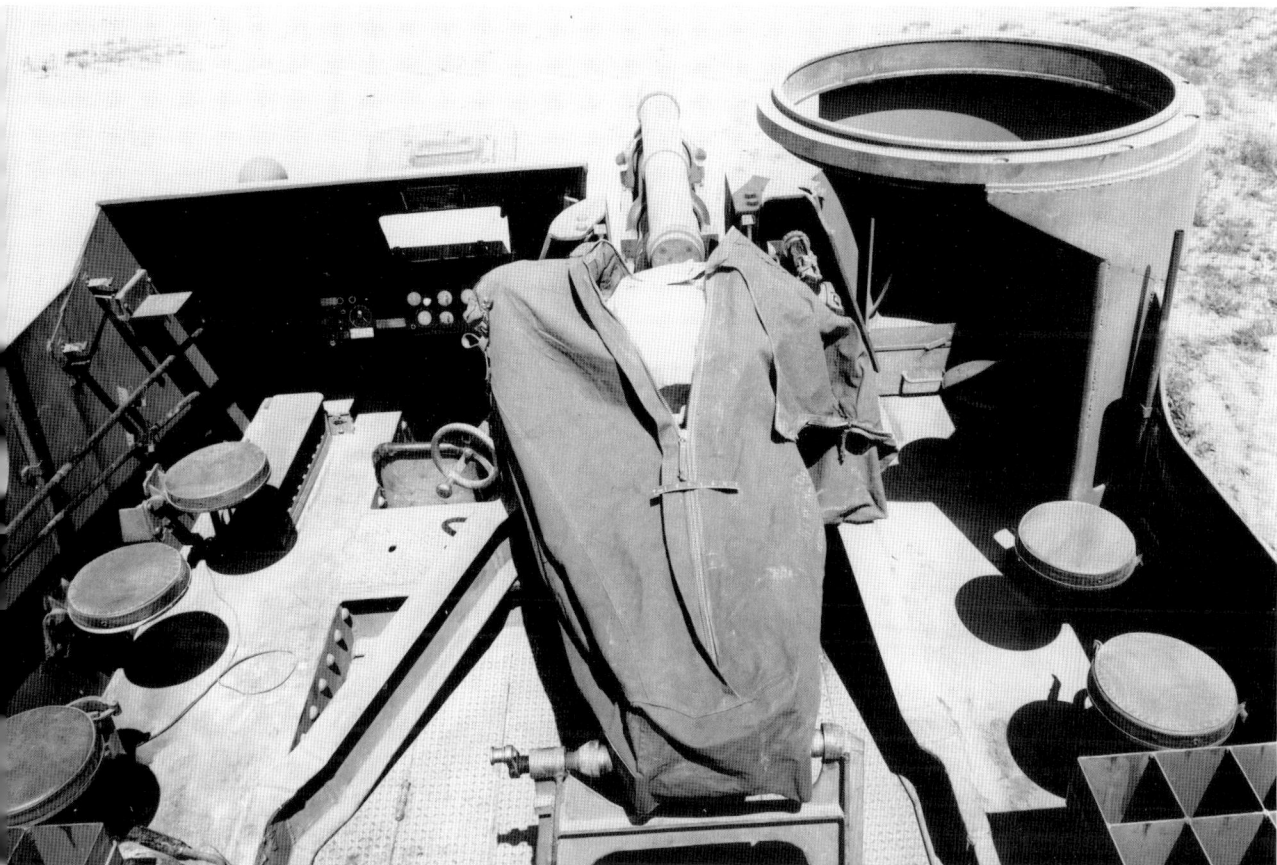

To the left of the howitzer in an M7 in this 20 August 1942 photograph is a Panoramic Telescope M12A2, mounted on a 6in extension to allow it to sight over the frontal armor. This telescope was used for sighting the howitzer for indirect fire. (NARA)

# Chapter Two

# American Locomotive Works
# M7

Track assemblies are being installed and adjusted on M7s at the American Locomotive Company (ALCO) plant in Schenectady, New York in January 1943. On the second tank, the track has been placed on the track-support rollers over the bogie frames, but the bogie wheels are still resting on the assembly-line floor. By this stage of production, a curved piece of armor had been placed on the side of the superstructure below the pulpit, yielding what is sometimes called the 'deep' pulpit. (*Library of Congress*)

(**Above**) A lone 105mm Howitzer Motor Carriage M7 on the American Locomotive assembly line next to several Medium Tanks M4 in January 1943. Note the horizontal weld line towards the top of the superstructure to the front of the pulpit, and the manner in which the edge of the frontal plate of the superstructure is exposed. (*Library of Congress*)

(**Opposite, above**) Small-hatch Medium Tanks M4 and early-production 105mm Howitzer Motor Carriages M7 are lined up at a special event for ALCO workers and guests in Schenectady on 10 April 1943. This was part of a series of events and ceremonies promoting the Allied war effort in North Africa. In the left background is a movie theater where the crowd was invited to see the US premier of the British documentary film *Desert Victory*, which featured some of the armored vehicles ALCO was producing. (*University of Memphis*)

(**Opposite, below**) The exhibition of M4 medium tanks and M7s in Schenectady is seen from an elevated position on Erie Boulevard. For some reason at this point in time, ALCO's publicity department was referring to the M7 as a 'tank killer' and the army sometimes referred to it as a 'tank destroyer', although the vehicle was intended mainly to provide mobile indirect-fire support. A close study of this image shows that by now, the tarpaulin racks on the rear decks of the M7 had been redesigned, with a long rack and two short ones on each side. There was a gap between the two short ones to accommodate a coiled tow cable. Also there was now a ventilation grille on the deck next to each sponson box, with a metal guard over the grille. The final drive assembly of the nearest M7 is the three-piece model used on early M4 medium tanks.

An M7 rolls down a city street during a parade or other exhibition. Three grouser boxes of various sizes are on the front of the vehicle. The sponson boxes had been redesigned; they now had a top lid with hinges on the inboard side and a padlock hasp on the outer edge. This photo gives a clearer view of the M4 medium tank-type three-piece final drive assembly. (*Efner History Research Library*)

Civilians, including several women inside the vehicle, get an up-close look at an M7. The placard wired to the tow shackles reads: 'M-7 GUN CARRIER | "Tank-Killer" | Built by | American Locomotive Company.' This early-production M7 features a single-piece cast final drive assembly. (*Efner History Research Library*)

This 8 May 1943 photograph of the front left corner of the driver's compartment of 105mm Howitzer Motor Carriage M7 Ordnance number 2477 documents the newly-relocated rifle brackets (left), Protectoscope stowage box (the small box at the center of the photo), and the bracket for the first-aid kit (above the front rifle bracket). To the upper right is the panoramic sight box, below which is a panel with the ignition switch and other switches. The driver's vision port is out of the view to the right. (NARA)

RESTRICTED

(**Above**) The tarpaulin for the fighting compartment is installed on this M7. This vehicle had headlights mounted in the early configuration, high on the frontal plate. The final drive assembly is the three-piece bolted type. The driver's visor is raised, showing the glass windshield and wiper installed. (*Patton Museum*)

(**Opposite, above**) The tarpaulin on the M7 is viewed from the left side. This vehicle had the solid-spoked bogie wheels, the trailing-type track-support rollers and no folding armor panels atop the superstructure sides and rear. (*Patton Museum*)

(**Opposite, below**) The M7 with the tarpaulin installed is viewed from the right side. Removable bows supported the rear and the center of the tarpaulin, while the top of the driver's compartment and the pulpit supported the front of the tarpaulin. (*Patton Museum*)

(**Above**) The tarpaulin over the fighting compartment of the M7 is viewed from the rear of the vehicle. At the center of the tarpaulin is a panel that is rolled up to allow ventilation or vision to the rear. Two straps are secured from the top of the tarpaulin to the rear deck. (*Patton Museum*)

(**Opposite, above**) A man in the driver's seat of an M7 is looking through the detachable windshield assembly. The windshield was detachable and was installed on the exterior of the hull with four clips, only when the visor was raised. Running across the glass are defroster wires. Details are visible of the interior of the raised visor and the underside of the howitzer cradle, including the elevation sector. Note the panoramic sight protruding through the tarpaulin above the driver's compartment. (*Patton Museum*)

(**Opposite, below**) The 105mm howitzer has been removed from its mount in this photo of the fighting compartment of an M7. Among the many details visible here are the two radio antennas mounted on the top of the driver's compartment, the driver's seat and instrument panel, the cradle for the 105mm howitzer (center), the travel lock for the howitzer (bottom center), and the ring mount (upper right). (*Patton Museum*)

An ALCO M7, Ordnance number 2718, is shown in a 25 March 1944 photograph taken for the Ordnance Operation, Engineering Standards Vehicle Laboratory, Detroit. The bogie assemblies remain the early type with the track-support roller centered above the bogie frame. The bogie wheels are the solid-spoked design. Sheet-metal fenders and sand shields are installed. The pulpit is the 'deep' type with a welded-on section below the level of the top of the superstructure. Two radio antennas are on top of the driver's compartment. (*Patton Museum*)

A late-production M7 is viewed from the left rear. Some of the late-model features include the folding armor panels on the sides and rear of the superstructure, the bogie assemblies with trailing track-support rollers, the stowage baskets on top of the sponson boxes, and the ventilation louvers on the sponson boxes. The bogie wheels are the smooth, concave type (drawing no. D52861). (*Patton Museum*)

# Chapter Three

# Federal Machine and Welder M7

Late in World War II, the E9 suspension was devised for M4 Medium Tanks and vehicles based on M4 chassis as a means for improved performance on soft ground and snow. This suspension included tracks with extended end connectors on both sides. To allow clearance for the inboard extended end connectors, spacers were installed on the hull for mounting the vertical volute suspension assemblies and idler assemblies, and extended final drives were installed. Federal Machine and Welder produced 176 M7s and 162 M7B1s with E9 suspensions in 1945, and it is believed that all of these vehicles had the E9 suspensions installed at the factory. This M7 is shown with a relocated tow pintle and trailer at Aberdeen Proving Ground on 6 June 1945. The only visual tipoff that this vehicle has the E9 suspension is the distinctive fender and braces that accompanied this suspension. (*NARA via Joe DeMarco*)

An M7 with E9 suspension of Battery A, 342nd Armored Field Artillery Battalion, drives past during the New York City Victory Parade on 12 January 1946. The extended end connectors on both sides of the track assemblies are clearly visible. The end connectors yielded a track that was 23-11/16 inches wide. Convex D78540 bogie wheels are installed, and the nickname "ABLES ACE" is on the side of the fighting compartment. (NARA via Joe DeMarco)

# Chapter Four

# Pressed Steel Car Company M7B1

Around the same time that the late-production M7s were under construction, the 105mm Howitzer Motor Carriage M7B1 was produced. It featured a Ford GAA tank engine and was based on the Medium Tank M4A3 chassis. The Pressed Steel Car Company manufactured the M7B1s, with a total of 826 produced from 1944 to 1945, and this example of the vehicle is seen outside that plant. *(Kenneth Nielsen, LTC, USA, Retired collection)*

In this photo of M7B1 Ordnance number 4366 taken at Aberdeen Proving Ground on 28 December 1944, the vehicle looks much like a late M7, except the rears of the sponson boxes did not come even with the rear of the sponson due to the slightly longer length of the hull. This was a key identifying feature of the M7B1. *(NARA)*

105mm Howitzer Motor Carriage M7B1 registration number 40152359, or Ordnance number 3896, is shown in a 25 September 1944 photograph. The rear decks of the M7B1s were very different from those of the M7s, having two large grilles/doors, but this feature is seldom seen to good effect in photographs. *(Patton Museum)*

This view of M7 registration number 4039645 shows how the rears of the sponson boxes were virtually flush with the rears of the sponsons. Visible inside the overhang at the rear of the upper hull are the air cleaners. The hinged armor panels on top of the superstructure are folded down. *(Patton Museum)*

The spaces on the tops of the sponsons to the rears of the sponson boxes, a feature of the M7B1, are clearly visible here. The extra space on the upper rears of the sponsons allowed space for installing taillight assemblies. The rear end of the M7B1 was totally different to that of the M7, with a large rear plate on the upper hull, below which was an exhaust-deflector grill. *(Patton Museum)*

This M7B1 was photographed during testing by the Armored Force Board at Fort Knox, Kentucky. The vehicle was marked with the number 751 on the side and the front of the pulpit. Rounded fenders and sand shields were installed on this vehicle. The headlight assemblies and their brush guards were in the late-production locations on the lower part of the frontal armor. (*Patton Museum*)

# Chapter Five

# Howitzer Motor Carriage M7B2

Based on experience in the Korean War, the 105mm Howitzer Motor Carriage M7B2 was developed. Based on the M7B1 chassis, the M7B2's howitzer was raised to above the top of the front of the superstructure in order to achieve a greatly-increased maximum elevation (+65 degrees: 30 degrees more than the elevation of the howitzer in the M7), allowing the piece to shell targets on the reverse slopes of nearby hills and mountains. In order to allow the ring-mounted machine gun a clear field of fire, the pulpit was built up as well. *(Patton Museum)*

The pulpit of an M7B2 is viewed from the rear. The structure was welded from numerous sections of curved plate. A crew seat was located towards the bottom of the pulpit. To the left are the 105mm howitzer breech and cradle. (*Patton Museum*)

The 105mm howitzer of an M7B2 is viewed from the left rear. The piece normally was fitted with a curved shield that traversed in unison with the howitzer, but that shield has been removed. Below the howitzer is the support structure for the piece, including the legs. (*Patton Museum*)

An M7B2 is seen from the left side. The basic vehicle's M7B1 pedigree is apparent in the space between the rear of the sponson box and the rear of the sponson. This vehicle reportedly was transferred to the Austrian Army after the Second World War. (*Patton Museum*)

# Chapter Six

# **Field Use**

Several soldiers are visible in the fighting compartment of an M7 at the American Maintenance School, a US Army Ordnance repair depot at Heliopolis, Egypt in September 1942. At this time, this base was involved in repairing US vehicles operating in British service under the Lend-Lease program, and British troops were trained here in repairing and servicing these vehicles. (*NARA*)

(**Above**) Some early-production M7s were issued with single-piece final drive assemblies with blunt, rounded front ends (as opposed to the sharper front ends that would appear on later-production FDAs), as seen in this photo taken at the Desert Training Center in September 1942. (*NARA*)

(**Opposite, above**) The same M7 at the Desert Training Center in September 1942 is viewed from the front left, with a Half-Track Personnel Carrier M3 next to it. This vehicle features the headlights in the early positioning, near the top of the frontal plates. No brush guards are present. Below the left headlight is the horn, also referred to as the siren. The thickness of the sheet-metal fenders is visible from this angle. (*NARA*)

(**Opposite, below**) A 105mm Howitzer Motor Carriage M7 is disembarking from a landing craft at a harbor in the Arzew Department of Oran, Algeria on 9 November 1942, the second day of Operation TORCH, the Allied invasion of French North Africa. Large recognition stars were painted on the rear and sides of the vehicle. This M7 had the ventilation grilles with steel guards on the inboard sides of the sponson boxes, and the sponson boxes were the early type with the access doors on the outboard sides. By now, in addition to the bin for twelve rounds of 105mm in each rear corner of the fighting compartment, to the fronts of these bins was a single row of additional bins and a close examination of this photo discloses that feature. (*NARA*)

(**Opposite, above**) The crew of this M7 in British service in North Africa in November 1942, registration number S169311, has just fired the 105mm Howitzer M2A1, the barrel, sleigh and recuperator assembly of which are in full recoil. Several months after this photo was taken, the British and Commonwealth forces would start operating the Sexton, a howitzer motor carriage similar to the M7 but mounting the Ordnance QF 25-pounder. (*Patton Museum*)

(**Above**) The British and Commonwealth armed forces received numbers of M7s, which they designated the 105mm Self-Propelled Gun, Priest. These are not to be confused with the similar-looking 25-pounder Self-Propelled Gun, Sexton, which had a different weapon. An example of a British or Commonwealth Priest is viewed close up. (*Allen County Historical Society*)

(**Opposite, below**) This photo of a British or Commonwealth Priest appears to be related to the vehicle and the location in the preceding photo, presumably in North Africa in late 1942. The vehicle has the typical, for the British, heavy load of bedrolls, tents, tarpaulins, liquid containers and packs stowed on rails and any available surface. The white-colored section on the forward part of the superstructure is not the camouflage paint, but a clumsy attempt at retouching for censorship purposes: note how the retoucher painted the rear end of one of the rolls. (*Allen County Historical Society*)

(**Opposite, above**) An M7 has become stuck in deep sand during a training exercise at Camp Young, better known as the Desert Training Center, in Southern California on 24 December 1942. Another M7 is parked on the rise behind the vehicle. Dust covers are installed on the headlight assemblies and the howitzer. Grousers are stored in the two large grouser boxes on the front left of the vehicle but not in the small box on the right-hand side. (*NARA*)

(**Above**) Crewmen in an M7 wait for their mates below to hand up ammunition in preparation for firing practice at the Desert Training Center in California on 7 January 1943. Markings on the upper right corner of the final drive assembly indicate that this vehicle was assigned to the 128th Armored Field Artillery Battalion, 6th Armored Division. (*NARA*)

(**Opposite, below**) Two M7s, one with a large recognition star and one without, are being employed in training maneuvers at Fort Sill, Oklahoma, home of the Field Artillery School, in February 1943. Vertically-positioned ammunition packing tubes are visible along the sides of the fighting compartments. This exposure of the tops of the ammunition left them very vulnerable to hits from bullets and shrapnel, but the army would soon devise a remedy for that deficiency. (*NARA*)

(**Opposite, above**) A 105mm Howitzer Motor Carriage nicknamed 'BIRMINGHAM BESS' pulling a trailer is positioned in a thicket during a training exercise at Fort Sill in February 1943. The trailer is a John Deere-produced Trailer, Armored, T32, which had hinged covers on top. (*NARA*)

(**Opposite, below**) Three M7s are firing salvoes during maneuvers at Fort Sill, Oklahoma in February 1943. All three vehicles have the early-type pulpits (with the bottom even with the top of the superstructure armor) and early-model bogie assemblies. At least the closest M7 has a single-piece final drive assembly. (*NARA*)

(**Above**) In another of the series of photos taken during maneuvers at Fort Sill in February 1943, an M7 emerges from the water after fording a stream. Without taking special deep-fording precautions, the M7 had a normal maximum fording depth of 40in. (*NARA*)

This photo of an early-production M7 was featured on the front cover of the March 1943 issue of *Firepower*, a magazine published jointly by the US Army Ordnance Department and the US Navy Ordnance Bureau. Inside that issue was an article on M7s titled 'Tank Destroyer', as the US Army was publicizing that these vehicles were going to assume the role of tank-killers; a role that never came to be in an organized, service-wide fashion. Painted on the superstructure is 'M7' over the number 156. Although the tracks are obscured by mud, enough of them are visible to identify them as T49s. (*NARA*)

The M7 in the foreground is poised in a gully during field artillery maneuvers at Fort Sill in February 1943, while another M7 is approaching in the background. On the side of the superstructure of the nearer vehicle is the nickname 'Bulls Eye 3'. (NARA)

(**Above**) The crew of an M7 has just fired the 105mm howitzer during maneuvers at Fort Sill, Oklahoma in February 1943. Unpacked 105mm rounds are in the bin at the right rear corner of the fighting compartment. Note the location of the identification star on the lid of the left sponson box; next to that box is the metal guard for a ventilation grille on the engine-compartment deck. (*NARA*)

(**Opposite, above**) The US Army began shipping masses of armored vehicles to Great Britain starting in 1942 in anticipation of the invasion of Nazi-occupied Europe. A 105mm Howitzer Motor Carriage M7 is engaged in training maneuvers outside of Tidworth, England on 23 March 1943. Recognition stars are painted on the side of the superstructure, on the bow and on the front of the machine-gun pulpit. (*NARA*)

(**Opposite, below**) During fighting in North Africa, the M7 often was pitted against the much-feared German 88mm gun, and in early 1943 both weapons were posed next to each other during comparative testing at Aberdeen Proving Ground, Maryland. According to the official army caption for this photo, 'Many German 88s have been knocked out' by the 105mm howitzers mounted on M7s. (*NARA*)

(**Above**) A Colonel Lillard and Brigadier General John O'Daniel confer with the driver of an M7 during rehearsals for the upcoming invasion of Sicily at Arzew, Algeria on 6 June 1943. A good view is available of the left fender and sand shield; particularly the serrated, bent edge of the fender where it is screwed to the front of the sand shield. Measures have been taken to waterproof the vehicle. The cover on the howitzer is watertight, being sealed to the weapon, and sealant material has been applied around the driver's vision-port cover. (*NARA*)

(**Opposite, above**) An M7 with waterproofing comes ashore at Arzew, Algeria on 6 June 1943 during a training maneuver in preparation for the invasion of Sicily. In addition to sealant material on the howitzer and its cradle and the driver's visor, a tarpaulin is lashed over the fighting compartment, and a deep-fording trunk is installed on the engine-compartment deck for taking in air for the engine and expelling exhaust. Note the small recognition star on the armor above the driver's compartment. (*NARA*)

(**Opposite, below**) M7s were present for Operation HUSKY, the Allied invasion of Sicily, in the summer of 1943. Here, an M7 rolls along a street in Palma di Montechiaro, Sicily on 7 July 1943. The recognition star on the side of the superstructure has a circle around it. The letter A is painted on the bow, and an indecipherable number is painted on the front of the pulpit. A bundle of camouflage netting is arranged on the front right side of the frontal armor. (*NARA*)

183981

179090

(**Opposite, above**) The recognition star on this M7 proceeding through Sciacca, Sicily on 20 July 1943 has a thin circle surrounding it, while the star on the side of the superstructure has a much thicker circle. The vehicle is towing an ammunition trailer. (*NARA*)

(**Opposite, below**) An M7 passes a group of welcoming civilians at Sciacca, Sicily on 20 July 1943. Including the driver, eight soldiers are present in the vehicle and one of them, to the rear, is wearing a tanker's helmet and goggles. (*NARA*)

(**Above**) This M7 photographed in Menfi, Sicily on 21 July 1943 may well win the prize for being loaded with the most equipment and supplies possible. Bedrolls, crates, camouflage netting and other items are piled high on the rear deck or lashed to the vehicle. On the left side of the body are non-standard holders for boxes, possibly for ammunition. (*NARA*)

196152

(**Opposite, above**) M7s are deployed to fire at a 'Red Force' anti-tank unit during Second Army maneuvers in Tennessee on 22 July 1943. The first and third vehicle, and probably the second one too, have trailers hitched to them. An illegible nickname is painted in white below the recognition star on the nearest M7. (*NARA*)

(**Opposite, below**) The 105mm howitzer of the M7 in the foreground has just been fired against German forces on Sicily on 7 August 1943. A trailer is hitched behind the M7. The troops in this photo had just been landed behind German lines and were attempting to capture an unidentified city. (*NARA*)

(**Above**) Following the capture of Sicily, the Allies invaded Italy in September 1943 and M7s saw extensive service in that campaign. Here, the M7 in the background is attempting to recover an M7 that has become stuck in a ravine on a mountain road near Caserta, Italy on 28 October 1943. Both vehicles have extension plates at the tops of the superstructure armor, but these are not the hinged plates with locking bolts seen later on M7s. Rather, they are an early type of arrangement, with the flush-mounted plates attached rigidly to the superstructure. (*NARA*)

(**Opposite, above**) An M7 of Battery A, 91st Field Artillery Battalion, performs a fire mission in the Mignano area of Italy on 30 December 1943; the barrel of the 105mm gun is in full recoil after firing a round. The vehicle has a camouflage scheme of the original Olive Drab paint with a lighter color, probably a tan or sand, on the front. To the far right is a stack of 105mm rounds in fiberboard packing tubes. (*NARA*)

(**Above**) To gain extra elevation for the 105mm gun during an indirect-fire mission, this M7 has been placed in a prepared excavation with the front of the hull up. The site was in the Rapido River area of Italy on 22 January 1944, and the vehicle was attached to an artillery company in an infantry regiment. A name is painted next to the recognition star, 'The Texas Special', with part of the name obscured by the circle around the star. (*NARA*)

(**Opposite, below**) This M7 of the 69th Armored Field Artillery Battalion is deployed for a fire-support mission to assist an operation of the 504th Paratroop Infantry Regiment in the Anzio area of Italy on 26 January 1944. This vehicle was nicknamed 'Carolina Moon'. On the lower front corner of the right side of the superstructure is painted the name 'CAROLINA' and artwork representing a crescent moon and stars. (*NARA*)

In March 1944 a column of M7s with the early-style machine-gun pulpits is proceeding along a British road during training maneuvers in preparation for the invasion of Normandy. Gunners are manning the .50-caliber machine guns in a defensive anti-aircraft stance. A wooden box with four compartments is on the rear deck of the first M7, and the photo provides an exceptional view of the components on the front end of that vehicle. The unit markings on the final drive assembly have been censored. (NARA)

(**Opposite, above**) A GI washes his feet with water in an M1 helmet next to an M7 named 'ANNA' and assigned to the 69th Armored Field Artillery Battalion. The scene was in the Anzio area on 2 February 1944. The 105mm gun of this vehicle has been in heavy use, as indicated by the piles of empty ammunition-packing tubes. A large roll of barbed wire is on the bow of the M7. (NARA)

(**Opposite, below**) M7s assigned to a tank battalion of the 45th Division are firing on enemy positions at the Anzio beachhead in February 1944. At least three M7s are in view, and all are positioned under camouflage nets rigged from poles stuck into the ground. (NARA)

(**Opposite, above**) Six M7s of the 22nd Armored Field Artillery Battalion are lined up at Prince Maurice Barracks, Devizes, Wiltshire, England on 18 March 1944. The first three vehicles have boxy fenders and sand shields, and at least the first M7 has the hinged top panels on the sides of the superstructure, replacing the rigid upper panels found previously on some M7s. The unit markings are stenciled on the pulpits; the first M7's markings stand for the twenty-third vehicle in the line of march of Battery B, 22nd Armored Field Artillery Battalion, 4th Armored Division. (*NARA*)

(**Opposite, below**) Shielded from enemy aircraft by a camouflage net, the crew of an M7 of the 191st Tank Battalion in the 45th Division area of the Anzio beachhead in Italy prepares to fire the 105mm howitzer at an enemy position. They have painted over the large star and circle on the vehicle in an effort to reduce its visibility. Note the remnants of a sand shield on the vehicle. (*NARA*)

(**Above**) M7s of the 321st Infantry Regiment, 81st Infantry Division, approach LST-486 during amphibious training exercises at Avila, California in March 1944. Later that year, that regiment would assist in the capture of Peleliu in the South-West Pacific. On the rear deck of the lead vehicle are a number of sheaves used in heavy-lifting operations. Below the pulpit is a square-shaped bridge-classification sign, 26 over 24. (*NARA via Sean Hert*)

(**Opposite, above**) Several M7s of the 321st Infantry Regiment, 81st Infantry Division, and a DUKW to the right await the word to begin embarking on LST-486 at Avila, California in March 1944. These are early-production M7s with early-style bogie assemblies, and lack the armored extensions at the top of the superstructure. (*NARA via Sean Hert*)

(**Opposite, below**) By early 1944, M7s were coming increasingly into use in the Pacific Theater. Here, an M7 splashes ashore after disembarking from Landing Craft, Tank 924 (LCT-924) during a practice session in advance of a landing operation on Guadalcanal on 11 March 1944. (*NARA*)

(**Above**) M7s are lined up in a field in the United Kingdom in preparation for the invasion of Normandy on 22 May 1944. All of them have been waterproofed, in part by adding sloped structures to the top of the fighting compartment to support tarpaulins. The closest vehicle, registration number 4037722, bears the nickname 'BABOON', followed by 4037948 'CHURCHILL' and 4038140 'CRIMSON TIDE'. What appear to be mine racks with mines stored on them are visible on the sides of the first two M7s. (*NARA*)

(**Opposite, above**) Brigadier General John W. O'Daniel came up with the idea of a 'battle sled': chains of one-man sleds that an armored vehicle could tow into position, giving the prone infantrymen some protection when advancing to attack fortified positions. Here an M7 is towing battle sleds in the Anzio area in Italy on 9 May 1944. A wooden crate and a wooden stowage bin are on a raised rack above the rear deck of the M7. (*NARA*)

(**Opposite, below**) The same M7 towing battle sleds in the Anzio area is viewed from the front on 9 May 1944. On the outboard side of the left headlight and brush guard is the bracket for the radio antenna. Markings on the final drive assembly are for the 1st Battalion, 30th Infantry Regiment, 3rd Infantry Division. (*NARA*)

(**Above**) Unit markings on the final drive assembly (FDA, otherwise known as the bow) of this M7 driving down a street in recently-liberated Carentan, France on 18 June 1944 indicate that it was assigned to Battery C, 14th Armored Field Artillery Battalion, 4th Armored Division. A large roll of hessian camouflage netting is stowed on the right fender. (*NARA*)

(**Above**) An M7 with the 105mm howitzer traversed to the right is approaching the photographer on a street in recently-captured Chiusdino, Italy on 27 June 1944. This is a late-production vehicle with a one-piece final drive assembly. The tracks appear to be the T48 type, with rubber track blocks with a chevron tread. (NARA)

(**Opposite, above**) There is no evidence of recognition stars on the bow or side of this M7 photographed as it drives through the ruins of the village of Roccastrada, about 56 miles south of Florence, Italy on 24 June 1944. (NARA)

(**Opposite, below**) Members of the crew of an M7 of Battery A, 27th Field Artillery Battalion clean the bore of the 105mm howitzer and reload the .50-caliber machine gun near Mensano, Italy on 2 July 1944. On the front of the pulpit is taped a sign on which is marked the weight, height, length and width of the vehicle. This M7 has the late-production configuration of headlights, relocated from the upper part of the frontal armor to the lower part. (NARA)

(**Opposite, above**) 83rd FA Bn 6th Armored Division Brest France 2 July 1944 The crew of an M7 nicknamed 'BEAR TRACKS' has rigged a canvas shelter along the side of their vehicle. They were members of the 27th Field Artillery Battalion, attached to the Fifth Army, and the site was at Mensano, Italy on 2 July 1944. This is an early-production M7 without the folding upper panels on the superstructure. (*NARA*)

(**Above**) This M7 of Battery C, 68th Armored Field Artillery Battalion, Fifth Army, was photographed while firing against a German counter-attack in the Montecatini area of Italy on 5 July 1944. The 105mm howitzer has just been fired and is in full recoil. Above the howitzer is a reel of communications wire. (*NARA*)

(**Opposite, below**) An M7 passes the grave of SS officer Josef Richtsfeld outside St-Gilles, France on 29 July 1944. The M7 is towing an Ammunition Trailer M10, and a large amount of gear is stowed on the rear deck. (*NARA*)

(**Above**) An early-type M7 of Battery B, 22nd Armored Field Artillery Battalion, 4th Armored Division, followed by an M4 Sherman medium tank, passes through the ruins of Coutances, France on 31 July 1944. There are two recognition stars on the final drive assembly of the M7; the lower one probably was painted on after the spare bogie wheel was mounted over the upper star. The disc-shaped object on the left fender is a bridge classification sign. (*NARA*)

(**Opposite, above**) Markings for Battery B, 66th Field Artillery Battalion, 4th Armored Division, are on the pulpit of this M7, passing through a town in France in July 1940. Affixed to the right fender is a bridge classification number 23. Oil cans are secured to the bow, and a spare bogie wheel is below the driver's vision port. In the left background is a knocked-out Light Tank M5A1. (*Jim Gilmore collection*)

(**Opposite, below**) An M7 of the 69th Field Artillery Battalion comes ashore from a landing craft near Mondragone, in the Naples area of Italy, on 31 July 1944. A deep-water fording trunk is visible towards the upper rear of the vehicle, and to make the vehicle further waterproof the howitzer has been elevated and a panel with proper sealing materials has been installed below it. (*NARA*)

(**Above**) The 105mm howitzer has just been fired on the No. 4 Priest of 'E' Troop, 78th Field Battery, 13th Canadian Field Regiment, Royal Canadian Artillery, 3rd Canadian Infantry Division during the Normandy campaign in July 1944. Note the additional side armor added to the superstructure alongside the fighting compartment. Later, this vehicle was converted into a Kangaroo armored personnel carrier by removing the howitzer and modifying the armor. (*Library and Archives of Canada*)

(**Opposite, above**) The same No. 4 Priest of 'E' Troop, 78th Canadian Field Battery, is seen from a closer perspective between firing shells at German forces in Normandy in July 1944. An ammunition box is stowed on the left grouser box, and the .50-caliber machine gun is fitted with a dark-colored dust cover. (*Library and Archives of Canada*)

(**Opposite, below**) The 105mm howitzer of a Priest of the 78th Canadian Field Battery is in full recoil while firing at German troops in Normandy in July 1944. A piece of supplemental armor plate is visible to the rear of the pulpit. The dark-colored feature in the right background is a pile of 105mm ammunition packing tubes. (*Library and Archives of Canada*)

(**Opposite, above**) In this view of the No. 4 Priest of 'E' Troop, 78th Canadian Field Battery, it is evident that there was no supplemental armor to cover the rear of the fighting compartment. On the sponson, the registration number is faintly visible: S-215880. (*Library and Archives of Canada*)

(**Opposite, below**) A Canadian Priest is in an excavated emplacement, its front end elevated to allow extra elevation for the howitzer. The tarpaulin has been pulled back from over the fighting compartment, but the bows that support the tarp are still in place over the compartment. (*Library and Archives of Canada*)

(**Above**) An M7 of Battery C, 39th Armored Field Artillery Battalion, 3rd Armored Division, pounds German forces near Saint-Pois, France on 3 August 1944. T48 rubber track blocks are in racks on the side of the fighting compartment. This vehicle has one of the later types of vertical volute spring suspension (VVSS) systems, with the track-support roller supported by arms to the upper rear of the bogie frame. (*NARA*)

(**Above**) In a field in the French countryside on 20 August 1944 US Army vehicles, including two M7s with trailers hitched to them, to the left and at the center, are assembling prior to resuming the push to the east. (*NARA*)

(**Opposite, above**) During the pursuit of retreating German forces following the break-out from Normandy, an M7 crosses steel treadways placed on a bridge over the Aisne River at Soissons, France on 30 August 1944. Racks for two 5-gallon liquid containers are on the fenders; the containers on the right-hand side are marked 'W' for water. (*NARA*)

(**Opposite, below**) General Mark Clark, commander of the Fifth Army, wearing a cap, watches as the 105mm howitzer of an M7 has just been fired at a German position in Italy on 24 August 1944. With Clark is Colonel Buttolph, commander of the 91st Armored Field Artillery Battalion. This vehicle, registration number 3034446, was part of the first ALCO production lot of 599 M7s. (*NARA*)

(**Opposite, above**) The barrel of the 105mm Howitzer M2A1 on an M7 is at almost full recoil after firing a round at a German strongpoint on the Gothic Line north of Lucca, Italy on 16 September 1944. The nickname 'Mable' is painted in script on the nearer M7, to the rear of the man speaking through the telephone handset. (*NARA*)

(**Above**) An M7 attached to the Seventh Army crosses a bridge to which members of the 36th Engineers are putting the final touches at Remiremont, France on 24 September 1944. To reduce the visibility of the vehicle to enemy gunners, the crew has painted over the recognition star with a dark-colored paint, possibly Olive Drab, contrasting with the weathered OD paint on the vehicle. Although this is an early-type M7, it has the late-type vertical volute bogie assemblies. (*NARA*)

(**Opposite, below**) Three identified crewmen are replenishing the 105mm ammunition in an M7 in the western frontier of Germany on 25 October 1944. They are, left to right: Private Charley Lillis of Atlanta, Texas; Sergeant Louis Braussard of Lafayette, Louisiana; and Corporal Willie D. Edwards of Refugio, Texas. (*NARA*)

195764

(**Opposite, above**) M7s saw considerable service in the US liberation of the Philippines in 1944–45. Here an M7 is firing phosphorus shells over a bridge near the approach to Toban, Luzon on 27 October 1944, to clear the way for troops of the 96th Division. (*NARA*)

(**Opposite, below**) The crew of an M7 with camouflage netting rigged over and behind it are on alert for enemy aircraft and troops somewhere in the European Theater on 29 October 1944. Faintly visible on the front of the pulpit are markings for Battery B, 253rd Field Artillery Battalion, Third Army. (*NARA*)

(**Above**) A GI to the right fires a bazooka at German forces in eastern France on 12 November 1944 as an M7 stands by to the left. A crewman in the pulpit has the .50-caliber machine gun trained towards the left side. The triangular shape to the front of the M7 is a poncho on a soldier. On the road in the background is another M7. (*NARA*)

(**Opposite, above**) On a cold, wet 17 November 1944 at Brulange, France, crewmen of Battery C, 276th Field Artillery Battalion, Third Army work in the mud to change a damaged track on an M7. This vehicle has a one-piece final drive assembly, late-type vertical volute bogie assemblies and an early-type pulpit. Note the two logs secured to the front of the vehicle. (*NARA*)

(**Above**) The front of the suspension of an M7 of the 231st Armored Field Artillery Battalion, 6th Armored Division, has been propped up with earth and pieces of wood to gain more elevation for the 105mm howitzer. The scene was a field outside of Kleinblittersdorf, Germany on 7 December 1944. A name painted on the side of the superstructure is partially hidden but appears to be 'ALL AMERICAN'. The nickname 'CRAZY HELEN' is painted on the barrel of the howitzer. Some 105mm rounds are stacked on the rear deck, and the hinged side panel of the superstructure is folded down. (*NARA*)

(**Opposite, below**) The crew of an M7 pauses to look at the photographer while shelling German positions along the River Rhine near Ribeauville, France on 9 December 1944. The crew's bedrolls are stacked on the rear deck. Note the pioneer tool rack on the side of the superstructure below the pulpit. On the ground are scores of packing tubes for 105mm ammunition as well as some 105mm rounds, the bases of their casings resting in the caps of the packing tubes to keep them off the ground. (*NARA*)

(**Opposite, above**) Some French artillery units were equipped with M7s, such as these examples of *5e Division Blindée, Première Armée Française*, which are shelling German positions in the Rhine valley around Kaysersberg, France on 17 December 1944. These 105mm howitzers have been engaged incessantly, as evidenced by the piles of hundreds of empty fiberboard packing tubes for ammunition. (*NARA*)

(**Opposite, below**) The same battery of M7s of *5e Division Blindée, Première Armée Française*, shown in the preceding photo, is viewed from a different angle while shelling German forces near Kaysersberg, France on 17 December 1944. These vehicles are marked with the tricolor red, white and blue national insignia. (*NARA*)

(**Above**) In another photo taken at Kaysersberg on 17 December 1944, an M7 assigned to *5e Division Blindée* is almost lost among the neat stacks and jumbled piles of empty fiberboard 105mm ammunition packing tubes. (*NARA*)

471509

(**Opposite, above**) In a final photo of *5e Division Blindée* operations at Kaysersberg, France on 17 December 1944, the crew of an M7 takes a break from shelling German forces in the Rhine valley. Large bundles of equipment are stowed on the rear deck of the vehicle. The ammunition box for the .50-caliber machine gun on the pulpit is painted white. (*NARA*)

(**Above**) During a routine inspection at the Unit Jungle Training Center on the island of Espiritu Santo, New Hebrides on 12 December 1944, a combined tank, infantry and artillery team moves forward. At the center is a 105mm Howitzer Motor Carriage M7, with 75mm Howitzer Motor Carriages M8 on its flanks and rear. A number 8 is above the star on the side of the superstructure of the M7. (*NARA*)

(**Opposite, below**) An M7 of Battery C, 274th Field Artillery Battalion, Third Army shells German troops outside of Bastogne, Belgium on 1 January 1945. This vehicle ran on stamped-spoke bogie wheels (drawing number C85163) and solid sprockets. Details of the interior side of the folding plate on the side of the fighting compartment are in view. (*NARA*)

(**Above**) An M7 is tucked under snow-covered camouflage netting in a photo taken somewhere in Europe on 8 January 1945. Empty fiberboard packing tubes for 105mm ammunition are neatly stacked to the right. A rather flimsy-looking rack has been added to the bow of the vehicle for retaining stowed gear; it is apparently fabricated from metal strips and rods. (*NARA*)

(**Opposite, above**) The crew of an M7 nicknamed 'ACROBAT III' of the Third Army prepares their 105mm howitzer for firing against German positions around Morhet, Belgium on 9 January 1945. Below the tarpaulin bow at the rear of the fighting compartment is a reel of communications wire on a spindle. Several ammunition trailers are in the field to the front right of the M7. (*NARA*)

(**Opposite, below**) A whitewashed M7 assigned to the 342nd Armored Field Artillery Battalion shells German positions in Geislautern, Germany on 24 January 1945. The whitewash was intended to camouflage the vehicle in snowy terrain. A tarpaulin rigged over the vehicle kept the crew and equipment in the fighting compartment dry and somewhat protected from the wind. (*NARA*)

199014

(**Opposite, above**) Sergeant Michael Perchak of Norwalk, Connecticut, a member of Battery C, 274th Armored Field Artillery Battalion, sits on a child's chair while he sets the fuse of a 105mm projectile. The scene was near Bastogne, Belgium on 5 January 1945. (*NARA*)

(**Opposite, below**) A column of M7s of the 2nd Armored Division moves forward toward Samrée, Luxembourg on 10 January 1945. The nearest vehicle, registration number W-4037797-S, was produced in November 1942 and has extra stowage racks on the rear of the hull. It also has mine racks on the side of the hull and two logs secured to the side. Visible on the tracks of the second and third M7s are 'duckbill' track extensions, which gave the vehicles extra flotation on snow and soft ground. (*Patton Museum*)

(**Above**) An M7 crew of Battery C, 398th Armored Field Artillery Battalion, prepares to fire a shell against a German position outside Wochern, Germany on 27 January 1945. Evidence of whitewashed camouflage is on the forward part of the 105mm howitzer, and two of the crewmen have whitewashed their M1 helmets. (*NARA*)

(**Above**) An M7 pulling an M10 ammunition trailer (right) enters a busy intersection in Bastogne, Belgium on 28 January 1945. The M7 shows evidence of a coat of deteriorating whitewash. A large amount of equipment, including crates and folded tarpaulins, is on the rear deck. A bicycle is lying on top of the tarpaulin on top of the ammo trailer. (*NARA*)

(**Opposite, above**) In the distance, an M7 picks its way through Victoria Street in the Intramuros section of Manila on 23 February 1945. The 105mm howitzer in the M7 had a devastating effect on Japanese strongpoints as US troops forced their way into the city. (*NARA*)

(**Opposite, below**) On the same day that the preceding photo was taken, an M7 blasts away at the wall of the Aquarium in Intramuros, which the Japanese were employing as a strongpoint. The vehicle is visible inside the enclosure to the left of center. (*NARA*)

(**Opposite, above**) At least a few M7s were stripped of their 105mm howitzers and given 9.75in mortar mounts around early 1945. Two such vehicles are shown during a demonstration in France on 28 February 1945. Developed by the British, this mortar was intended to fire incendiary rounds against German defenses along the Westwall. (*NARA*)

(**Above**) US Army Ordnance technicians 'deprocess', or unpack and prepare for service, an M7 that has arrived at the port of Rouen, France around February 1945. They are removing wooden packing from over the fighting compartment. The two recognizable GIs are Technician Fourth Grade Otto Sevin, left, and Technician Fifth Grade William G. Shaw. (*NARA*)

(**Opposite, below**) A lone M7B1 with an ammunition trailer, part of the 10th Armored Division, US Third Army, negotiates an M2 steel treadway bridge over the River Saar at Saarburg, Germany on 26 February 1945. A common practice, as seen here, was to place a wooden or metal beam between the front fenders to act as a retainer for stowed items, whether they were packs, bedrolls, liquid containers or boxes. A large amount of equipment is stowed under tarps on the rear deck. (*NARA*)

(**Opposite, above**) Troops of the 130th Infantry Regiment accompany an early-production M7 assigned to the 775th Tank Battalion during a patrol into the town of Naguilian, Luzon on 23 March 1945. The M7 is being used as a battle taxi, carrying some of the infantrymen on the rear deck. (*NARA*)

(**Opposite, below**) An M7 of Battery C, 22nd Armored Field Artillery Battalion, 4th Armored Division, Third Army crosses a pontoon bridge over the River Main near Hanau, Germany on 28 March 1945. Several wooden beams have been attached to the front of the hull to act as a retainer for a collection of boxes, liquid containers and other gear. An extra machine gun, a Browning .30-caliber M1919, has been mounted over the driver's compartment. (*NARA*)

(**Above**) In Limburg, Germany, on 27 March 1945, an M7 of Battery A, 73rd Armored Field Artillery Battalion, 9th Armored Division rounds a corner, coming face-to-face with a small-hatch Sherman medium tank. Two spare bogie wheels, an open-spoke type and a solid-disk design, are stowed on the final drive assembly. (*NARA*)

The 105mm howitzers of the M7s eventually wore out and had to be replaced. Here, with assistance from a truck-mounted boom, the crew of a late-production M7 of the 35th Division is swapping-out the howitzer at Nieukerk, Germany on 5 March 1945. This piece had fired some 5,000 rounds and as the bore wore out, the rounds it fired were falling shorter and shorter. Next to the right point of the recognition star is written in Old-English script 'Merry Widow'. Note the German *stahlhelm* (steel helmet) resting on the headlight brush guard. (NARA)

The crew is preparing to fire the 105mm howitzer of an M7 assigned to the Armored School Demonstration Regiment during a training exercise at Fort Knox, Kentucky, in 1943. Nicknamed 'FINALIST', this was an early-production M7, manufactured under the first contract for that type of vehicle. It had the two grilles with steel covers on the sides of the engine deck and the shallow pulpit. Note the bright red paint or primer on the inner part of the front of the pulpit.

*(National Archives)*

Members of the Armored School Demonstration Regiment serve the weapons on the M7 nicknamed 'FINALIST' at Fort Knox in 1943. The nickname is stenciled between the rungs. The registration number is visible at the rear of the sponson: 3034487. As was appropriate for an early M7, the headlights and blackout marker lamps are high up on the frontal armor. No brush guards are present to protect the headlights.

In an original color transparency, the 105mm howitzer of an M7 is firing during a training exercise in 1943. On this early-production M7, the headlights are supplied with brush guards. Faintly visible on the front of the pulpit is a unit marking, mostly covered by leaves. What appears to be the number 79 is on the right side of the marking. (*National Archives*)

Two M7 Priests (one is visible in the left background) attached to the Blue Force, 5th Armored Division, were photographed during war games along Highway 70, outside of Lebanon, Tennessee, on 5 May 1943. The Panoramic Telescope M12A2 is installed on its mount on the right side of the howitzer and is in view above the driver's vision port. (*National Archives*)

'FINALIST', M7 Priest registration number 3034487, presents its right front aspect during an exercise at Fort Knox in 1943. On the front of the pulpit is the folded-down travel lock of the .50-caliber machine gun. On the final-drive assembly is stenciled in white the unit marking: 'Δ S-DR F-X-2', the first part referring to the Armored School Demonstration Regiment. This unit, established in January 1942, was a smaller version of a U.S. Army armored division and was tasked with performing demonstrations of the operational functions of an armored division as well as training students in armored warfare. (*National Archives*)

(**Opposite, above**) The crew of 'FINALIST', M7 registration number 3034487, are shown mounted in marching order. The chief of section is standing; the gunner is to his front at the panoramic telescope; No. 1 cannoneer is at the pulpit machine gun, and cannoneers Nos 2, 3, and 4 are seated to his rear. The remaining crewman, the driver, is not in view. (*National Archives*)

(**Opposite, below**) The 105mm howitzer of an M7 Priest has just fired to dramatic effect during a firing exercise, either at dawn or twilight. The chief of section is standing in the vehicle with his arm raised; next to him is the gunner. This is an early M7, based on the positions of the headlights and brush guards, high up on the frontal armor. (*National Archives*)

(**Above**) During exercise Long Horn at Fort Hood, Texas, on April 8, 1952, an M7 from the 68th Field Artillery, 1st Armored Division, advances down a trail to take up a position against the Aggressor Force. A tight-fitting fabric cover is over the muzzle of the 105mm howitzer. (*NARA*)

(**Opposite, above**) This excellently preserved M7 Priest in the armored vehicle collection of Allan Cors is painted in a Tan and Olive Drab camouflage. It has a mix of bogie-wheel types, including open-spoke, stamped-spoke, and smooth concave.

(**Opposite, below**) Five footman loops are welded to the side armor of the M7, with an upswing toward the front. Two of the loops are on the upper part of the circle surrounding the star. These were for securing a tarpaulin over the fighting compartment. A bow for the tarpaulin is stored on brackets on the side armor.

(**Above**) The Cors M7 is captured in a three-quarter left-rear view. The panoramic sight, installed on the left side of the howitzer mount, protrudes above the breech end of the howitzer. The upper rear plate of the hull is an early-production type, the bottom of which has a stepped design.

(**Above**) The M7 has reproduction markings for Battery C, 91st Field Artillery Battalion, 1st Armored Division, in the Second World War. The T74 tracks mounted on this vehicle are of composite design, with rubber on the inner side. The exhausts are below the upper 'step' of the upper rear plate of the hull.

(**Opposite, above**) The Cors M7 Priest has the early-type pulpit, without the curved piece of armor welded to the bottom of the outboard side of the pulpit. The storage boxes were tack-welded to the rear deck; four weld beads are present on the outboard side of the box. The drive sprocket is the solid-steel 'economy' variant.

(**Opposite, below**) This M7 Priest formerly in the collections of Aberdeen Proving Ground has the curved, semicircular armored fillet extending about a foot below the top of the superstructure. The machine-gun cradle is still mounted in the pulpit. A hinged armor plate is on the top of the superstructure to the rear of the pulpit. Ventilation louvers are on the front and the side of the storage box on the rear deck, and a storage bin made of angle iron and expanded-steel mesh is mounted on the lid of the box.

This M7B1 Priest belonging to Greg Wolanin is painted overall in Olive Drab camouflage. Made by the Pressed Steel Car Company and based on the M4A3 Medium Tank chassis, this vehicle was powered by a Ford GAA tank engine.

The M7B1 is observed from the left side. Note the perforated steel strips welded to the bottom of the super-structure, for fastening skirts. As is often the case with preserved and restored vehicles derived from M4 Sherman chassis, each of the VVSS bogie frames (the suspension structures with vertical ribs) is of a different pattern, with varying mold seams and foundry marks.

Like the M4A3 Sherman it was derived from, the M7B1 features large, grille-type engine-access doors on the rear deck; a large rear-upper-hull plate with a straight bottom edge; and exhaust deflectors on hinges just below the bottom of the rear plate.

The Wolanin M7B1 has reproduction markings for Battery A, 493rd Field Artillery, 12th Armored Division. Spare track links are stored in the box-shaped holders on the front of the superstructure. On the front of the pulpit is a travel lock for the machine gun.

(**Above**) This M7B1 Priest is equipped with T48 tracks, with rubber treads with chevron grousers. Details of the headlight assemblies, the siren, and the brush guards are in view. The driver's visor is in the open position.

(**Opposite, above**) The forward end of the fighting compartment and the driver's station of the M7B1 are viewed from above. On the inside of the left side of the superstructure are, from the foreground forward, shell storage racks, a folding seat, rifle brackets, and a first-aid kit. The instrument panel is set at an angle for the driver's ease. Above that panel is the storage case for the panoramic sight, which, when in use, was mounted on the left side of the howitzer cradle.

(**Opposite, below**) The pulpit and its support structure on the M7B1 are shown. Below the pulpit are three rifle brackets. Below the front of the pulpit are storage racks for .50-caliber ammunition boxes as well as a box of tools for the .50-caliber machine gun. On the front of the ring of the pulpit is the rolling carriage for mounting the machine gun.

In a snowy field is an M7B2 that was in the collection of the late Fred Ropkey. The M7B2 was based on the same chassis as the M7B1, but the M7B2's 105mm howitzer was positioned above the superstructure, enabling it to be elevated to +65 degrees, 30 degrees more than that of the M7's howitzer. This facilitated shelling targets at very close range.

In order to permit the unobstructed operation of the .50-caliber antiaircraft machine gun on the M7B2, the pulpit was extended to above the howitzer. A canvas weather cover is attached to the top of the pulpit.

Even at the low perspective from which this left-rear view of the Ropkey M7B2 was taken, the 105mm howitzer and the upper part of the pulpit are still visible. The hinged armor panel on the top of the side of the superstructure has been unlocked and lowered.

The nickname 'Black Widow' and pinup art of a reclining lady are painted on the superstructure of the Ropkey M7B2. The bogie wheels on this vehicle are all the D385012 open-spoke type with steel plugs welded over the openings.

The 105mm howitzer and its mount in the M7B2 are viewed from the left rear. To the left front of the howitzer mount is the left side of the curved shield that traversed in unison with the howitzer. To the right of the howitzer is a folding seat. A Browning M2HB .50-caliber machine gun is mounted on the pulpit.

The right side of the 105mm howitzer is viewed, with the breech at the upper right, elevation hand wheel below and to the rear of the breech, and the gunner's seat at the center. To the front of the seat is the traversing hand wheel. In the left background is the driver's compartment.

In a view of a fully-loaded Landing Ship, Medium (LSM) in the Pacific off Oahu on 9 May 1945, five M7s are present. They are in staggered position on deck, alternating on the right side and the left side, in each case with a Half-Track Personnel Carrier M3A1 to its side. Markings are visible on the M7s' pulpits for Batteries A and B of the 428th Armored Field Artillery Battalion. This ship was operating in coordination with the Waianae Amphibious Training Center on Oahu. (NARA)

(**Above**) An M7 with the nickname 'SUPER RABBIT' painted to the front of the recognition star on the side of the vehicle crosses a bridge on the island of Panay in the Philippines on 18 March 1945. This is an early-production vehicle, with a three-piece final drive assembly, early-type bogie assemblies and no folding armor panels on the sides of the superstructure. (*NARA*)

(**Opposite, above**) Having just landed on Luzon in the Philippines, two M7s of the 158th Cannon Company, 158th Regimental Combat Team, proceed through the ruins of the town of Legaspi on 1 April 1945. Both vehicles exhibit the early-type upper-rear plates on the hulls, featuring stepped bottom edges. On late-production M7s, the upper step of the notch was filled in. (*NARA*)

(**Opposite, below**) The crew of a well-entrenched M7 assigned to the US Army's 25th Division blasts away point-blank at a Japanese pillbox at a range of 250 yards in the Balete Pass, Luzon, Philippine Islands, on 8 April 1945. The registration number, W-4039654, is visible on the sponson. Ready rounds of 105mm ammunition are stacked on the rear deck. The second man from the right is communicating by a telephone handset. (*NARA*)

(**Above**) An M7 of the 126th Cannon Company fires at Japanese positions on the Villa Verde Trail, Luzon on 12 April 1945. Although the registration on the side of the sponson is indistinct, it is clearly W-403xxxx, which pertains to a vehicle from ALCO's second production block of M7s. (*NARA*)

(**Opposite, above**) The barrels of their 105mm howitzers set to a little over 0 degrees elevation, several M7s are firing at Japanese strongpoints in a draw near Highway No. 9, Baguio, Luzon on 24 April 1945. The nearest M7 has early-type bogie assemblies, a hinged upper panel on the superstructure and the early three-piece final drive assembly. (*NARA*)

(**Opposite, above**) In a photo related to the preceding image, the crew of an M7 assigned to the 37th Division observes the effect of a 105mm shell they have just fired at a Japanese position along Highway No. 9 on Luzon on 24 April 1945. The bedrolls and other gear piled on the rear deck are on a wooden pallet stretching between the tops of the two sponson boxes. (*NARA*)

(**Above**) This Priest has turned perpendicular to Highway No. 3 near Baguio, Luzon in order to engage Japanese positions which were taking US infantry under fire on 16 April 1945. The troops were advancing from Banangan to Bagui, and from the shell casing littering the ground, at least a dozen 105mm rounds have been used to quash enemy positions. (*NARA*)

(**Opposite, above**) This 14 April 1945 photo of the interior of an M7 at Manila shows modified ammunition racks on both sides of the fighting compartment, facing the rear. The compartmentalized bins were removed and new racks were installed in which unpacked 105mm rounds were laid flat, presumably allowing more rounds to be carried. (*NARA*)

(**Opposite, below**) The modified ammo racks in the left side of the fighting compartment of the M7 at Manila are seen from above the breech of the 105mm howitzer. A laterally-mounted steel plate separated the rear rack and the front rack. The rear rack had bent-rod brackets to retain the ammo, while the front rack had a bent-rod retainer bracket with a piece of sheet metal welded to it. (*NARA*)

(**Above**) The modified ammunition racks are viewed from yet another angle. The front rack did not have a retainer at the front end to keep the rounds from shifting in that direction. (*NARA*)

(**Opposite, above**) There was only one modified rack on the right side of the M7 photographed at Manila on 14 April 1945. It had two bent-rod brackets on the inboard side and a lateral plate at the front. To the front of that plate are two portable fire extinguishers and a pair of shovels. Behind the cowl to the lower right is the engine-oil cooler. The howitzer is traversed to its maximum left limit. (*NARA*)

(**Opposite, below**) Different modified ammunition racks are displayed in this photograph. In this M7, there is a rear rack over the engine-oil cooler. It is of welded steel construction, with dividers for individual rounds in it. On the left side of the fighting compartment are two racks, full of packed 105mm ammunition. These racks are made of welded steel, with retainer strips on the inboard side of the racks. The rear rack held twenty rounds and the front rack fifteen. (*NARA*)

(**Above**) This M7 and crew have just landed on a beach on Okinawa in April 1945. Above the driver's compartment is an unusual feature: an armor shield with a single vision slot in the center of it. On the outboard side of the shield is what appears to be a .30-caliber machine-gun barrel. (*NARA via Sean Hert*)

(**Opposite, Above**) While operating in mountains outside of Manila in April 1945, this M7 rolled out of control down the slope, becoming mired 450ft below the road. In this photo, taken on 24 April, eight days after the recovery operation began, a tank retriever with a 30-ton winch is slowly pulling the vehicle up the slope. (*NARA*)

(**Opposite, Below**) The same M7 is viewed from the rear on 24 April 1945 as it is being pulled up the hillside by a winch on a tank retriever. Ammunition packing tubes are visible in the bins in the fighting compartment. An axe is stored on the upper rear plate of the hull. This was an early-production vehicle without the hinged plates on the top of the superstructure. (*NARA*)

(**Above**) Colonel Victor Bleasdale's 29th Marines move up to Ghuta, Okinawa on April 1945. Two M7s and, to the rear, a Sherman tank are performing extra duty as battle wagons, transporting members of the 29th Marines to Ghuta, Okinawa, in April 1945. On the nearer M7, closely-arranged rubber track blocks have been fastened to the side of the superstructure, most likely for additional protection against projectiles, shrapnel and magnetic mines. (*Patton Museum*)

(**Opposite, above**) In late April 1945, elements of the Fifth Army were attempting to seal off German forces attempting to escape from Italy into Austria and Switzerland by way of Lake Garda in northern Italy. This early-production M7 was photographed while shelling German forces around Lake Garda on 30 April 1945. (*NARA*)

(**Opposite, below**) An M7 is pounding away at retreating German forces along Lake Garda from a vacant lot in the town of Malcesine, Italy. Note the tow cable wound around the rungs on the side of the fighting compartment. In the left background is a local landmark, Castello Scaligero. On the street to the far left is another M7. In the foreground, artillerymen are unpacking and preparing 105mm ammunition. (*NARA*)

(**Opposite, above**) Jeeps and trucks have pulled to the side of a narrow dirt road to allow two M7s to pass during combat operations in the Davao Region of Mindanao, the Philippines, on 4 May 1945. The space is so narrow that a shirtless GI on the road is signaling the driver of the M7 so he doesn't hit another vehicle. (*NARA*)

(**Above**) At a shop in the European Theater on 29 May 1945, army technicians inspect waterproofing that has been applied to an M7. A box-like structure has been mounted over the pulpit and across the top of the howitzer; the muzzle of the howitzer is covered and sealant has been swabbed on the howitzer shield, closing the gap between it and the howitzer. (*NARA*)

(**Opposite, below**) A mud-spattered M7 is proceeding to the front lines at Shuri, Okinawa on 31 May 1945. It was named in memory of Ernie Pyle, the famous and very popular war correspondent who had recently been killed during fighting on nearby Ie Shima. In addition to the normal pulpit-mounted .50-caliber machine gun, this vehicle has a field-mounted Browning M1919 .30-caliber machine gun with a small shield above the driver's compartment. (*NARA*)

(**Above**) The 105mm howitzer of an M7 of the 1st Marine Division is in full recoil as it fires against a Japanese position on Okinawa in May 1945. Although difficult to discern, the entire side of the vehicle is covered with track sections for additional protection. (*Patton Museum*)

(**Opposite, above**) In a photo related in time and place to the preceding image, two 1st Marine Division M7s with tracks attached to their sides are in a firing position on Okinawa on 12 May 1945. Both vehicles have deep-fording trunks mounted on their rear decks. Between the two vehicles, artillerymen are sitting and standing on a trailer. (*Patton Museum*)

(**Opposite, below**) During the battle for Rangoon, Burma between March and May 1945, the 105mm howitzers of three Priests are pounding Japanese positions along one of the roads leading to Rangoon. An illegible nickname is painted on the side of the first vehicle, next to the driver's compartment. Steel chevron tracks are installed on at least the first two Priests. (*NARA*)

(**Above**) The 637th Tank Destroyer Battalion employed M7s during their combat operations on Luzon, the Philippines. Here, an M7 of the 637th has just forded the Magat River on Luzon, en route to Crodon on 12 June 1945. In the background, an M20 utility vehicle and several M18 tank destroyers pass knocked-out Japanese trucks as they prepare to cross the river. (*NARA*)

(**Opposite, above**) M7s of Battery C, 78th Field Artillery Battalion, US 2nd Armored Division fire a forty-eight-round salute in honor of Independence Day in Berlin on 4 July 1945. The nearest fully-visible vehicle, registration number W-4038604-S, bears the nickname 'COMING HOME' below the pioneer tool rack. The second M7 is registration number W-4039518-S. (*NARA*)

(**Opposite, below**) To enable the 105mm howitzer to fire at very close targets, the weapon mount on this M7 was modified to enable the piece to fire at a very high angle. The photo was taken in Korea on 15 March 1951. (*NARA*)

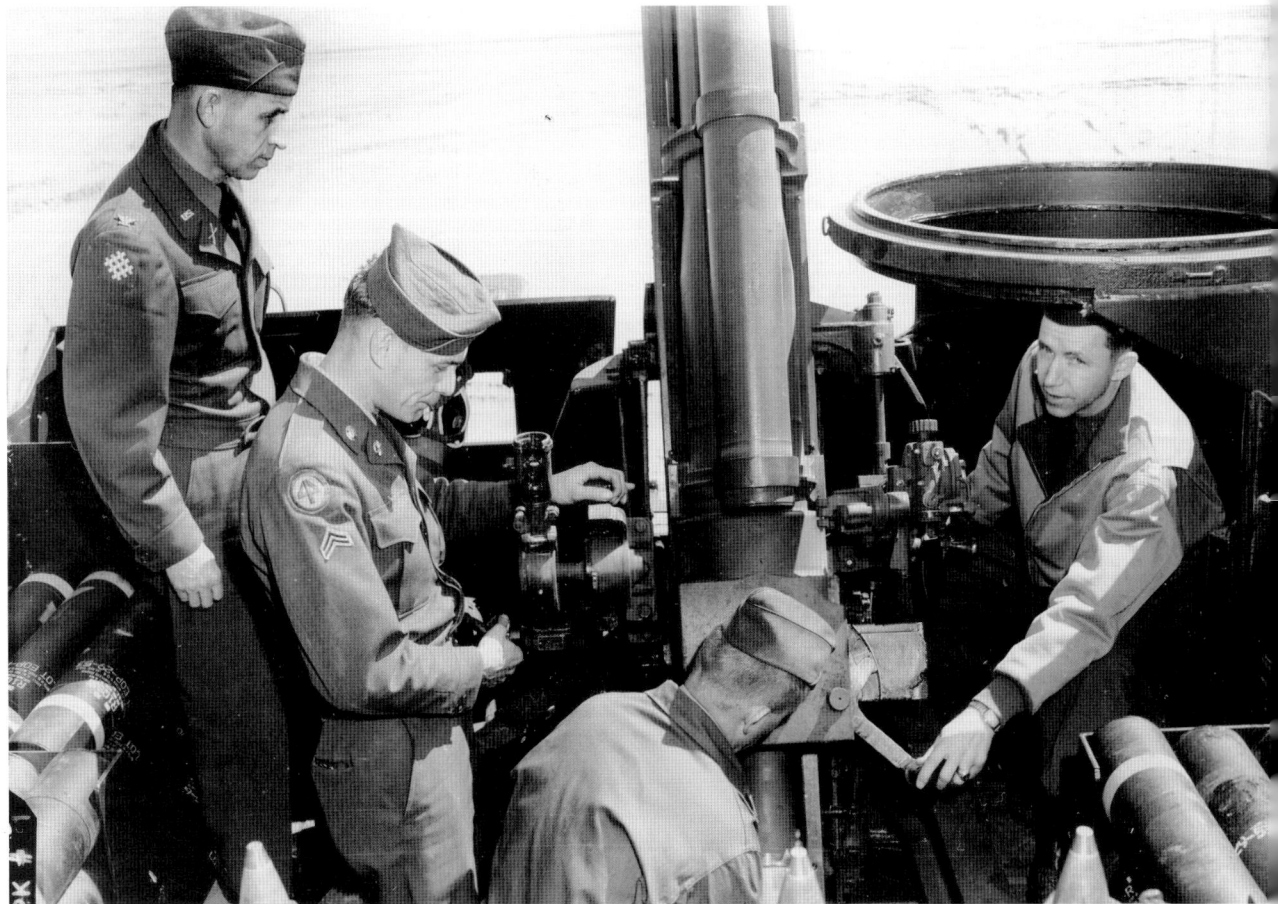

(**Opposite, above**) The M7 that was modified in Korea to permit the howitzer to fire at a high angle was fitted with a modified travel lock on the deck to the front of the howitzer shield. The travel lock is shown here engaged to the howitzer cradle on 15 March 1951. (*NARA*)

(**Opposite, below**) The crew of an M7 modified to fire its 105mm howitzer at a higher than normal elevation is preparing the piece for firing in Korea on 15 March 1951. This vehicle was furnished with the modified ammunition racks that allowed for the horizontal stowage of rounds in the rear corners of the fighting compartment and the storing of vertical rounds between those racks. (*NARA*)

(**Above**) An M7B1 passes troops of the 19th Infantry Regiment, 24th Infantry Division, during an advance in Korea on 23 April 1951. Although the original caption for this photo identifies this M7B1 as attached to Company D, 6th Armored Battalion, 24th Division, the only armored unit numbered 6th that was attached to the 24th Division at that time was the 6th Medium Tank Battalion. (*NARA*)

(**Opposite, above**) Members of the 1st Howitzer Platoon, Battery B, 213rd Armored Field Artillery Battalion, IX Corps are firing the 105mm howitzer of an M7B1 at enemy positions north of Kapyong, Korea on 25 May 1951. The word 'Babe' and a painting of a pin-up girl are on the side of the pulpit. Ammunition is stacked on the rear deck of the M7B1, and a large load of equipment is on a wooden rack on the rear of the vehicle. Below that rack is the exhaust-deflector grill that was a key feature of the M7B1. With its longer hull, the M7B1 also was characterized by a space on the rear deck aft of each sponson box, a feature not present on the M7s. (*NARA*)

(**Opposite, below**) An M7B1 of Battery C, 300th Field Artillery Battalion, US Eighth Army provides fire support to troops of the 1st US Marine Division during the battle for Hill 785 in Korea on 22 September 1951. The registration number on the sponson is 40152627. A tarpaulin has been partially erected over the fighting compartment as a sunscreen. Note the stowage rack installed on the rear of the hull. (*NARA*)

(**Above**) 'CASSINO' is the nickname painted on the side of the driver's compartment of this M7 of Battery C, 91st Anti-Aircraft Field Artillery Battalion, 1st Armored Division, during Exercise Long Horn, a joint US Army-US Air Force maneuver at Fort Hood, Texas on 30 March 1952. The registration number on the sponson is 4040048, a late-production ALCO vehicle. (*NARA*)

A tank retriever is being positioned to haul off a disabled half-track to the left while another tank retriever to the right is about to tow away a damaged M7 in Korea on 17 July 1953. The crews of the half-track and the M7 had disabled them to prevent advancing Chinese troops from putting them to use. Note the ammo packing tubes stored horizontally in the right side of the M7's fighting compartment. (*NARA*)

Members of an M7 crew of Battery B, 161st Armored Field Artillery Battalion (Kansas National Guard) prepare to fire a round during a training exercise at Camp Carson, Colorado on 17 August 1954. The vehicle, registration number 40152402, has artwork on the superstructure next to the driver's compartment: the nickname 'Bouncin Betty', above which is a painting of an artillery shell in flight, upon which is a bee or hornet with a human head. (*NARA*)

# Appendix One

# Priest Contracts and Deliveries

### American Locomotive Company M7

Contracts as listed in 'Armored, Tank and Combat Vehicles, 1 May 1945', prepared by the Records Section, Statistics and Analysis Branch, Stock Control Division, Office of Chief of Ordnance, Detroit.

   599 units W-740-ORD-485 PO T-3529
     RN 3034235 thru 3034833; SN 3 thru 601
   2,714 units W-740-ORD-485 PO T-3882
     RN 4037519 thru 4040232; SN 603 thru 3316

Subtotal from Armored, Tank and Combat, Vehicles May 1945: 3,313

Deliveries by ALCO as listed in Summary Report Tank-Automotive Material Acceptances January 1946:

   PO T-3529   600 in 1942
   PO T-3882   1,428 in 1942; 786 in 1943; 500 in 1944; total 2,714

Deliveries as listed in 'Recapitulation of Facility Expansions for Tracked & Wheeled Vehicles from 1940 to July 15, 1945', prepared by the Special Planning Branch, Office of Chief of Ordnance, Detroit.

| | | | | | |
|---|---:|---|---:|---|---:|
| April 1942 | 38 | January 1943 | 124 | March 1944 | 60 |
| May | 29 | February | 194 | April | 52 |
| June | 58 | March | 0 | May | 48 |
| July | 152 | April | 175 | June | 85 |
| August | 290 | May | 75 | July | 65 |
| September | 179 | June | 75 | August | 76 |
| October | 101 | July | 75 | September | 76 |
| November | 615 | August | 68 | October | 38 |
| December | 566 | Sept–Dec | 0 | Nov–Dec | 0 |
| Subtotal '42 | 2,028 | Subtotal '43 | 786 | Subtotal '44 | 500 |
| | | | | **Total** | 3,314 |

## Federal Machine and Welder M7

Contracts as listed in 'Armored, Tank and Combat Vehicles, 1 May 1945', prepared by the Records Section, Statistics and Analysis Branch, Stock Control Division, Office of Chief of Ordnance, Detroit.

259 units 303-33-019-2242 PO T-15511
RN 40190383 thru 40190641 SN 4911 thru 5169
300 units 303-33-019-2242 PO T-15511
RN 40192091 thru 40192390 SN 5170 thru 5469

Subtotal from Armored, Tank and Combat, Vehicles May 1945: 559

Deliveries by Federal Machine and Welder as listed in Summary Report Tank-Automotive Material Acceptances January 1946:

PO T-15511 176 in 1945, total 176

Deliveries as listed in 'Recapitulation of Facility Expansions for Tracked & Wheeled Vehicles from 1940 to July 15, 1945', prepared by the Special Planning Branch, Office of Chief of Ordnance, Detroit.

| | |
|---|---|
| March 1945 | 5 |
| April | 22 |
| May | 50 |
| June | 50 |
| July–Dec | 0 |
| **Subtotal** | 127 |

## Pressed Steel Car Company M7B1

Contracts as listed in 'Armored, Tank and Combat, Vehicles 1 May 1945' prepared by the Records Section, Statistics and Analysis Branch, Stock Control Division, Office of Chief of Ordnance, Detroit.

628 units W-271-ORD-717 PO T-10154
RN 40152252 thru 40152879 SN 53384 thru 54011
198 units W-271-ORD-717 PO T-10813
RN 40172420 thru 40172617 SN 4417 thru 4614

Subtotal from Armored, Tank and Combat, Vehicles May 1945: 826

Deliveries by PSC as listed in Summary Report Tank-Automotive Material Acceptances January 1946:

PO T-10154 628 in 1944; total 628
PO T-10813 36 in 1944, 162 in 1945; total 198

Deliveries as listed in 'Recapitulation of Facility Expansions for Tracked & Wheeled Vehicles from 1940 to July 15, 1945', prepared by the Special Planning Branch, Office of Chief of Ordnance, Detroit.

| | | | | |
|---|---|---|---|---|
| March 1944 | 42 | January '45 | 150 |
| April | 47 | February | 12 |
| May | 49 | Subtotal '45 | 162 |
| June | 49 | | |
| July | 69 | **Total PSC** | 826 |
| August | 69 | | |
| September | 85 | | |
| October | 79 | | |
| November | 77 | | |
| December | 115 | | |
| Subtotal '44 | 664 | | |

# **General Data**

| Model | M7 | M7B1 |
|---|---|---|
| Weight* | 52,000 lbs | 50,000 lbs |
| Length | 222 9/32 ins | 243 3/4 ins |
| Width | 113 5/16 ins | 113 5/16 ins |
| Height | 104 ins | 102 ins |
| Track | 83 ft | 83 ft |
| Std Track Width | 16 9/16 ins | 16 9/16 ins |
| Crew | 7 | 7 |
| Maximum Speed | 24 mph | 26 mph |
| Fuel Capacity | 176 gallons | 168 gallons |
| Range | 85 miles | 85 miles |
| Electrical | 24 volt negative ground | 24 volt negative ground |
| Transmission Speeds | 5 (forward), 1 (reverse) | 5 (forward), 1 (reverse) |
| Turning Radius | 31 ft | 31 ft |
| Armament Main | 105 mm | 105 mm |
| Armament Flexible | 1 × .50 in (caliber) | 1 × .50 in (caliber) |
| Engine Make/Model | Continental R975-C1 | Ford GAA |
|    Number of Cylinders | 9 radial | V-8 |
|    Cubic Inch Displacement | 973 | 1,100 |
|    Horsepower | 350 @ 2,400 rpm | 500 |
|    Torque | 840 @ 1,700 rpm | 1,100 |
|    Governed Speed | 2,400 rpm | 2,600 rpm |

* Fighting weight.

## **Communication Equipment**

The Priest carried a M238 flag set.

# Appendix Three

# M2A1 Howitzer Specifications

Bore: 105mm (4.134 inches)
Length (muzzle to rear face of breech): 101.35 inches (24.5 calibers)
Length of bore: 93.05 inches
Length of rifling: 78.02 inches
Length of chamber (to rifling): 15.03 inches
Rifling: 36 grooves, RH twist, 1 turn in 20 calibers
Breechblock: Manual, horizontal sliding wedge
Weight: 1,080 pounds
Maximum rate of fire: 8 rounds per minute
Maximum pressure: 28,000 psi
Muzzle velocity: 1,250 fps (HEAT-T) to 1,550 fps HE, smoke
Maximum range: 8,580 yds (HEAT-T) to 12,205 yds (M84 smoke)

| Ammunition weights (lbs): | Complete round | Projectile only |
|---|---|---|
| HE M1 | 42.07 | 33.00 |
| M67 HEAT-T | 36.85 | 29.22 |
| M60 WP Smoke | 43.77 | 34.31 |
| M84 HC Smoke | 41.94 | 32.87 |

# Appendix Four

# **Armored Field Artillery Battalion**

## Headquarters and Headquarters Battery

Personnel: 14 officers and 97 enlisted men.
Equipment and vehicles:

Two L-4 Liaison Aircraft
Three M4 Medium Tanks
Ten Half-tracks (M3 or M3A1)

One 2.5-ton Truck
Two 1-ton Cargo Trailers
Nine 0.25-ton Jeeps

## Service Battery

Personnel: 5 officers, 2 Warrant Officers and 86 enlisted men.
Equipment and vehicles:

Two Armored Recovery Vehicles
(M31, M32, M32B1 or M32B3)
One 10-ton Heavy Wheeled Wrecker
(M1 Series)
Twenty-one 2.5-ton Trucks

Twelve 1-ton Cargo Trailers
Nine M8 or M10 Ammunition Trailers
Two 0.75-ton Dodge Trucks
One 0.75-ton Dodge Command Car
Three 0.25-ton Jeeps

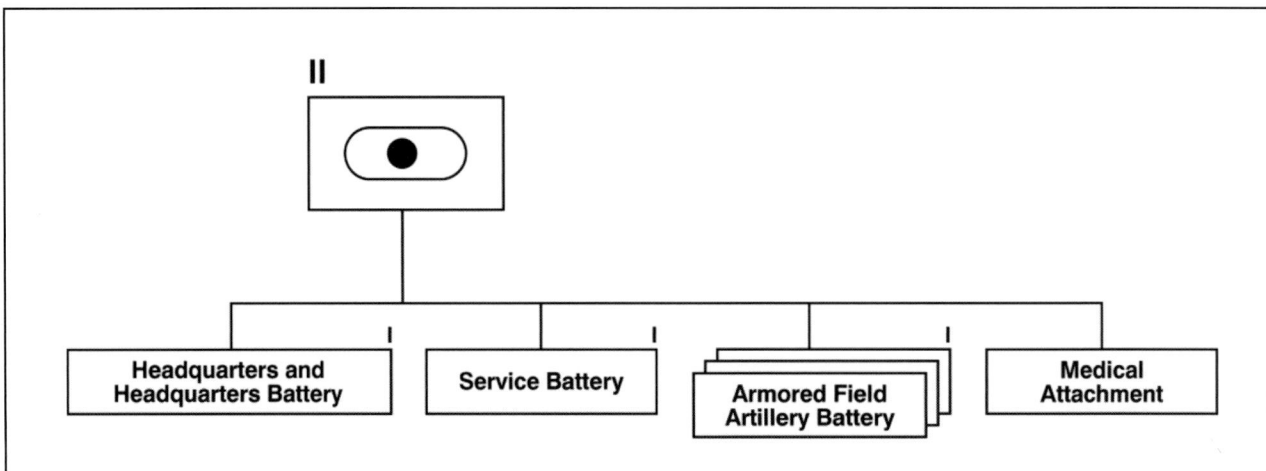

```
                    II
                 ┌───────────┐
                 │  ⬭ ● ⬭   │
                 └─────┬─────┘
                       │
      ┌────────────┬───┴────┬──────────────┐
┌───────────┐ ┌──────────┐ ┌────────────┐ ┌──────────┐
│Headquarters│ │ Service  │ │ Armored    │ │ Medical  │
│    and     │ │ Battery  │ │ Field      │ │Attachment│
│Headquarters│ │          │ │ Artillery  │ │          │
│  Battery   │ │          │ │ Battery    │ │          │
└───────────┘ └──────────┘ └────────────┘ └──────────┘
```

## Armored Field Artillery Battery (3)

Personnel: 4 officers and 106 enlisted men.

Equipment and vehicles (each battery):

| | |
|---|---|
| Six M7 105mm HMC | Eight M8 or M10 Ammunition Trailers |
| Seven Half-tracks (M3 or M3A1) | Three 0.25-ton Jeeps |
| One 2.5-ton Truck | Two 0.25-ton Trailers |
| Two 1-ton Cargo Trailers | |

## Medical Detachment

Personnel: 1 officer and 10 enlisted men.

Equipment and vehicles:

| | |
|---|---|
| One M3 Half-track Ambulance | One 0.25-ton Trailer |
| One 0.25-ton Jeep | |